BARBECUE
COOKBOOK

Alison Holst

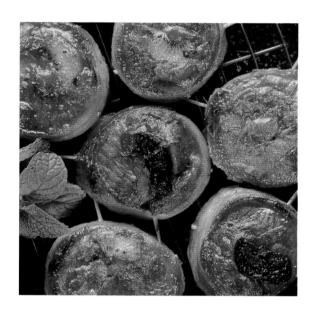

C. J. Publishing

First published in 1996 by
Chanel Publishers Ltd T/A C. J. Publishing
P.O Box 70, Newport Beach, NSW 2106

This edition published for Cobra Import Export Pty Ltd
No. 6 City South Business Park
16–34 Dunning Avenue
Rosebery, NSW

Copyright © Alison Holst

ISBN 0-908808-68-2

Publisher: Cliff Josephs
Author: Alison Holst
Editor: Renée Lang
Designer/Production: Sue Attwood
Printed through Bookbuilders, Hong Kong

Contents

Introduction

**There is a lot of truth in the saying
that food seems to taste better outdoors and, without
a doubt, your barbecue will entice you outdoors,
liberating you from many kitchen chores.**

What better way to enjoy a long, balmy evening than to relax outside while an informal meal sizzles over the coals. The simplest of food will taste so much more interesting outside than it would do indoors.

It is a pity to limit your barbecues to evening meals. Enjoy leisurely weekend breakfasts, brunches and lunches with your family and friends around this versatile appliance, instead of entertaining them in other more expensive and elaborate ways. Barbecues shouldn't only mean meat. Starters, vegetables, salads and breads are important parts of the meal, too. As you develop your barbecue skills, you may find that you are using your barbecue for several different foods at each meal. Your only problem may be keeping everyone's appetites in reasonable bounds. Barbecued food smells and tastes so good that it disappears very fast!

The information in this book should help you to use your barbecue efficiently to cook a range of foods. It gives particular emphasis to foods that cook in a relatively short time, and which are suitable for everyday family meals and casual entertaining. Although some foods require cooking on solid plates, most of the recipes are designed for cooking on grill racks, so their slightly smoky barbecue flavour can be emphasised and enjoyed.

When you cook on a gas or electric barbecue, you can choose to have the food plainly grilled or give it a smoky flavour, to a greater or lesser degree. On a rack just above the gas flames or electric elements, you can place a layer of lava rock (scoria), or a layer of pumice, or of small ceramic bricks. The gas or electricity heats these until they glow and radiate heat. When juice from food drips onto them, it sizzles and smokes, and the smoke gives the food its 'barbecue' flavour.

You can increase this smoky flavour by putting soaked hardwood chips on top of the hot rocks. The wet chips smoke, rather than burn, and this extra smoke gives the food on the rack above a more marked flavour. If you cover the cooking food with a tent of heavy aluminium foil, or with the domed lid that is sold with some barbecues, you surround it with a warm atmosphere, and it cooks more quickly. You also trap the smoke formed by the juices falling on the hot coals or from the smoking hardwood chips, so you intensify the smoky flavour.

The lava rock, pumice, and ceramic bricks may be re-used many times. However, you will need a new supply of soaked hardwood chips each time you barbecue.

If you like a smoky flavour to your food, but do not want to add it by burning aromatic wood, you can use smoke-flavoured seasonings instead, adding them to marinades, sauces, or simply sprinkling the cooked foods with them. A number of these are available, but you may have to hunt for them. I use a product called Liquid Smoke, an American flavouring in a bottle, which is readily available here. It is a dark-coloured liquid that is added to other liquids, drop by drop. A related American product is a smoke-flavoured spray which can be applied directly to food. Consider also Hickory Smoked Salt, a grey-coloured salt with a good smoky flavour. Look for it in spice shelves in supermarkets.

There are various dry mixtures available for sprink-ling onto foods to give them a barbecue flavour. Some of these are smokier than others, and may be worth investigating if you cannot find the first-mentioned products.

Foil-wrapping enables many low-fat foods to be heated on the barbecue in a steamy atmosphere so that they do not burn before they have cooked. They do not have a browned surface or a barbecued flavour, unless they are unwrapped and browned over the hot rocks/embers after they are tender.

A griddle or heavy flat plate cooks food by pan-grilling. This food has little or no smoky flavour. Many foods which can not be cooked directly on a rack can be cooked on a hot plate. Your kitchen is kept free from spatters and heat, and the outside clean-up time will probably be considerably less.

Heavy pots, pans and kettles can be used on a barbecue, too. In this situation, as when using the griddle, the barbecue is being used as an outdoor stove-top. The food will taste much the same as it would if cooked indoors. You may cook some foods in heavy pots earlier in the day and bring them outside to heat up on the barbecue and serve with your other barbecued foods.

Recipes for various marinades, glazes and sauces appear throughout the book. However, for easy reference a number of them, especially marinades that are suitable for all cuts of meat, fish and chicken, are grouped together in a separate chapter.

Alison Holst

Barbecue Cooking Times

It is not possible to give exact cooking times for particular foods, because so many factors affect the cooking time:

- air temperature
- wind speed and direction
- starting temperature of food
- size and thickness of pieces of food
- distance between the food and the heat
- whether food is uncovered or covered
- the amount of fat removed from meat
- degree of cooking preferred.

In general, small pieces of food can be cooked at high heat. Large pieces of food need a lower heat so that the outside does not burn before the inside of it is cooked.

Testing "Doneness"

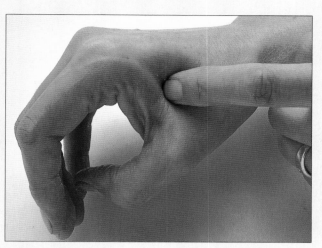

Rare, or underdone steaks feel soft and spongy, as when you relax your hand and press the area between thumb and hand.

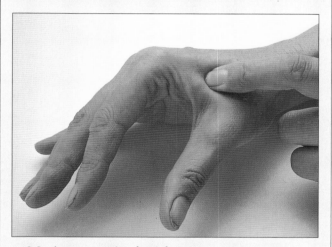

Medium steaks feel firmer and springier, as it feels if you flex your fingers and press the same area.

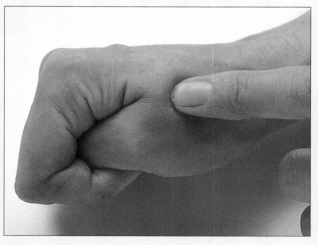

Well done steaks feel very firm (and may be tough) as when you make a tight fist and press the same area.

Popular Poultry

Chicken barbecues beautifully! Whether you cook it very simply or dress it up for guests, poultry is always a popular barbecue choice, hard to beat for versatility, economy and good nutrition.

Although you can barbecue chicken in any form, it makes sense to concentrate on chicken which has been 'broken down' into smallish, flattish pieces, since these will cook more easily, evenly, and quickly than a whole chicken, chicken halves, or a chicken that has been opened flat. You will find a good selection of chicken pieces in any supermarket. Chicken cuts that have been skinned and boned cook the fastest. Chickens are always young and tender, so you do not have to worry about tenderising the flesh, although you may want to marinate it for extra flavour.

Chicken skin – on or off?

Chicken skin, although crunchy and delicious, is much fattier than the flesh underneath it and can burn readily.

If you cook skinless chicken pieces, this problem does not arise. And if you precook the chicken (usually in a microwave oven) just brown it, in a shorter time, on your barbecue.

Barbecued chicken breasts

Boneless, skinless chicken breasts are readily available, and may be barbecued whole, or cut in pieces and threaded on a skewer. They cook very quickly, may be marinated for flavour, and should always be brushed with oil or melted butter before they are cooked.

Although you do not want to lose too many juices, you should pierce the flesh deeply, at intervals, and remove the breasts from the heat as soon as the juice runs clear, rather than pink. Depending on the heat of the barbecue, this can be a little as 4 minutes per side.

Barbecued chicken legs

Thighs and drumsticks on the bone are thicker than breast meat and take longer to cook. It is easier to cook them without burning the outside if you either skin or precook them first. Without precooking, they may take up to 30 minutes to barbecue. They are ready when the juices run clear, not pink. (To precook, microwave each thigh for 2 minutes and each drumstick for 1 ½ minutes on High (100%) power.)

Boneless chicken thighs

Look for boneless, skinless chicken thighs. Opened flat, they cook very quickly, sometimes as quickly as 2 minutes per side. Marinate them in a mixture containing some oil, and brush with extra marinade or with a glaze as they cook. The flesh is moist and especially delicious.

Chicken wings

Chicken wing pieces cook faster than drumsticks since they are small. They have a high proportion of skin to flesh, and may drip more than you want if not precooked. From a raw state they may take 20 minutes or longer to cook.

Handy Hint

You can always tell when chicken is cooked by removing it from the barbecue, then piercing the thickest part with a sharp knife. As soon as the juice runs clear, not pink, the chicken is cooked.

Red-Cooked Chicken

Red-Cooked Chicken

When you have a large number of people to cook for, it is worth finding ways to 'speed up operations'. Precooking chicken in this strongly flavoured sauce means that it needs only reheating on the barbecue. Cooking times are reduced enormously, and you should have no problems with fat flare-ups.

4 chicken legs
1 cup cold water
½ cup dark soy sauce
½ cup light soy sauce
2 tablespoons sherry
walnut-sized piece fresh ginger, peeled and sliced
1 clove garlic, peeled
1 star anise 'flower'
1 ½ tablespoons sugar

To precook the chicken, combine all the ingredients, adding chicken legs last, in an unpunctured oven bag. Microwave on High (100% power) for 12–14 minutes, turning pieces in the bag two or three times, or until juices are no longer pink when thighs are pierced deeply. Or simmer in the marinade in a covered pan for 15–30 minutes, turning once or twice. Test as above.

Pour off cooking liquid, strain and refrigerate for re-use within a week or freeze it for later use.

Barbecue the chicken on a rack soon after precooking or refrigerate until required. The chicken may be barbecued quite close to the heat since it is already cooked and only requires heating through.

Serve hot with barbecued fresh vegetables, warmed bread rolls and a leafy green salad. Serves 4.

Barbecued Chicken Kebabs

If you find it difficult to judge when a whole chicken breast is cooked, you may prefer to make kebabs instead. You can make good chicken kebabs by threading cubes of skinless chicken breast, or cubes of boneless skinless chicken thigh meat, onto soaked bamboo skewers. Marinate them in your favourite mixture, then barbecue them for a short time. Brush kebabs with olive oil or melted butter, or with a mixture of 1 tablespoon each of honey, lemon juice and oil, warmed together, or with Lemon Butter Baste (see opposite). Oil the grill rack or spray it with non-stick spray. Place kebabs fairly close together on the hottest part of the grill rack,

cook for 2 minutes, then turn and cook for 2 minutes longer. Kebabs are cooked as soon as they feel fairly firm when pressed, and when a cube of chicken, cut in half, has no translucent uncooked part in the middle. The kebabs should be lightly browned, and marked with dark lines from the hot rack, if the barbecue was hot enough to start with. Cook for a little longer if necessary, but take care not to overcook since the lean breast meat, which is very tender and moist if cooked to the right stage, dries out quickly if it is overcooked.

Kebabs with the honey glaze will be darker brown than those brushed with butter or oil.

Lemon Butter Baste
Finely chop or crush a large clove of garlic. Heat with 1 tablespoon butter until butter bubbles. Stir in 2 teaspoons light soy sauce or fish sauce and 1 tablespoon lemon juice. Brush on chicken or fish before and during cooking.

Variations: Try the various glazes used in the other chicken recipes in the book when making kebabs.

Sesame Chicken

These small pieces of chicken are marinated before they are cooked – for colour as well as flavour. They make a good addition to a buffet, on any festive occasion, and may be eaten as fingerfood.

300 g chicken wings or drumsticks, approximately
2 tablespoons soy sauce
2 tablespoons sherry
1 tablespoon sugar
1 tablespoon sesame oil
1 clove garlic, finely chopped
2 tablespoons toasted sesame seeds

Put the prepared chicken pieces in an unpunctured heavy-duty plastic bag, then add all the remaining ingredients except for the sesame seeds. (Use dark soy sauce for a browner glaze.) Leave for 5 minutes to 24 hours.

Barbecue on a rack for about 20 minutes, turning and brushing with remaining marinade several times during cooking. When you think the chicken is cooked, pierce the thickest piece. If the juices run pink, cook longer until juices run clear.

Sprinkle with toasted sesame seeds straight after cooking. Serves 2.

Mexican Chicken

This tasty and popular chicken is very easy to make using a home-made seasoning mix.

6–8 skinless, boneless chicken thighs
  or 4 chicken breasts
1 teaspoon butter
1 teaspoon oil
2 tablespoons Mexican Coating Mixture

Ensure that all skin and bone is removed from chicken. Bang chicken breasts between two pieces of cling film, using a rolling pin, until they are 1 cm thick. Make sure that thighs will lie flat, snipping meat if necessary. Brush with, or turn in, a mixture of melted butter and oil.

Five–10 minutes before cooking, sprinkle the chicken on both sides with Mexican seasoning, using quantities to suit your taste (about a teaspoon per side for each piece gives a good flavour).

Barbecue on a rack close to the heat until juices no longer run pink when the flesh is pierced in the thickest place.

Slice thighs diagonally before serving, if you like. Serves 6.

Mexican Coating Mixture

If you like the flavour of the herbs and spices used in Mexican cooking, mix them in a screw-topped jar so you have them on hand. Use to flavour chicken for a quickly prepared meal.

1 tablespoon paprika
1 tablespoon oreganum
1 tablespoon ground cumin
1 tablespoon onion or garlic salt
1 tablespoon flour
2 teaspoons caster sugar
1 teaspoon chilli powder, approximately

Mix all the ingredients, crumbling leaves of oreganum, if you like. Use less chilli powder for less hotness. Store in an airtight container. Makes about ⅓ cup.

Above: Mexican Chicken
Below: Sesame Chicken

9

Sesame Soy-glazed Chicken Thighs

This is my favourite family chicken barbecue recipe. It requires next to no preparation, is amazingly quick to cook, and tastes delicious. Gone are the days of charred skin and under-done insides.

    6–8 skinless, boneless chicken thighs
    3 tablespoons light soy sauce
    2 tablespoons sesame oil
    1 teaspoon finely chopped garlic
    fresh parsley or coriander, and lemon
      wedges to garnish

Put the chicken pieces in a bowl with the remaining ingredients. Leave to stand for about half an hour if possible, or for at least 5 minutes.

Barbecue on a rack for about 3 minutes each side on a preheated barbecue. When the meat is pierced in the thickest part and no pink liquid emerges, then the chicken is cooked.

Leave to stand in a warm place for 5 minutes, then place on a board and cut each thigh into about 5 diagonal slices. Arrange these on a serving plate, garnish with parsley sprigs (or fresh coriander leaves) and lemon wedges if desired, and serve hot or warm.

This chicken is good dropped into pockets of pita bread, or served on rice or noodles with a spoonful of chicken juice spooned over it. Serves 4.

Quick Chicken Satay Sticks

This is a good way to turn a couple of chicken breasts into a quick, interesting meal for two.

    2 skinless, boneless chicken breasts
    1–2 tablespoons lemon or lime juice
    1 tablespoon each soy sauce and fish sauce
    1–2 teaspoons sesame oil
    1 teaspoon ground cumin
    2 cloves garlic, finely chopped
    1 teaspoon grated fresh ginger
    1 tablespoon chopped coriander leaves
      (optional)
    1 cup satay sauce, bought or home-made

Soak 12 bamboo skewers in cold water.

Cut the chicken breasts lengthways into 1 cm strips. Place strips in a bag with all the remaining ingredients, except the satay sauce. Leave to marinate from 5 minutes to 24 hours, as time allows.

Thread the chicken strips lengthways onto the skewers and barbecue on a rack close to the heat until cooked, 3–5 minutes each side (juice should run clear when chicken is pierced). Serves 2.

Quick Satay Sauce

Brush small amounts of this sauce over chicken pieces before cooking.

    ½ cup chopped roasted peanuts
    4 pieces crystallised ginger
    1 tablespoon brown sugar
    ½ teaspoon ground coriander
    2 cloves garlic, chopped
    juice of 1 lemon
    2 tablespoons light soy sauce
    3–4 drops Tabasco sauce
    1 tablespoon oil
    1 cup coconut milk

Using a food processor or blender, chop the first five ingredients together until very fine, then add the next four ingredients and process again. Gradually add the coconut milk until the sauce is the consistency of thin gravy. Heat until it boils and thickens.

Sesame Soy-glazed Chicken Thighs

Greek Barbecued Chicken

Greek Barbecued Chicken

What better way to enjoy long summer evenings than to barbecue chicken with this definite Greek flavour!

4 large or 8 small bone-in chicken pieces
juice of 1 lemon
¼ cup olive or other oil
1 teaspoon paprika (optional)
2 cloves garlic, crushed
1 teaspoon oreganum

Choose chicken legs or quartered chickens for this recipe, or thread wings or small pieces on skewers for easier turning during cooking. If necessary, break joints so pieces lie flat. Put chicken with all the remaining ingredients in an unpunctured plastic bag. Allow to stand for 30 minutes, turning bag occasionally.

Cook chicken on a rack, 15–20 cm from the barbecue heat, or turn down the heat so that it cooks slowly and evenly. Chicken should be ready in 20–30 minutes, or as soon as juices run clear, not pink, when flesh close to bone is pierced.

Serve with a Greek salad, plenty of bread, and with grapes for dessert. Serves 4.

Cuban Chicken

Interesting marinades from other parts of the world make lean, skinned, boned chicken breasts really exciting. Lime juice and coriander leaves make this chicken unforgettable!

4 skinless, boneless chicken breasts
3 cloves garlic, finely chopped
½ teaspoon ground cumin
¼ teaspoon oreganum
¼ teaspoon thyme
1 tablespoon finely chopped fresh
  coriander leaves
3 tablespoons lime juice
3 tablespoons olive oil
1 teaspoon sugar
½ teaspoon salt

Pat chicken breasts dry with absorbent paper, trim if necessary, then place one breast between a folded plastic bag on a board. Bang evenly and gently with a rolling pin until breast is one and a half times its original size. Place in a sponge roll tin big enough to hold all of the chicken in one layer. Prepare the other breasts in the same way.

Mix the remaining ingredients together in a screw-top jar or combine them using a food processor. Brush mixture over both sides of the prepared chicken and leave to marinate for at least 15 minutes or up to 24 hours in the refrigerator, covered with cling film.

Preheat a heavy barbecue plate. Brush or rub with a film of oil, then cook the chicken until brown on each side and just cooked in the middle. This should take only 2 minutes per side if you have beaten the chicken out thinly.

Serve with Spicy Bean and Rice Salad (see page 60). Serves 4.

Cuban Chicken

Tandoori Chicken

This popular Indian dish is best prepared ahead and left in its marinade overnight (or at least for 1–2 hours). It cooks with little last-minute fuss.

3–4 cloves garlic
½ cm root ginger, grated
½ teaspoon chilli powder
1 teaspoon ground cumin
1 teaspoon coriander
1 teaspoon paprika
1 teaspoon turmeric
1 teaspoon garam masala
1 teaspoon mint
1 teaspoon salt
1 cup unsweetened yoghurt
8 small or 4 large chicken pieces (skin removed for preference)

Crush and chop the garlic and grate the ginger. Combine with all of the spices, mint and salt in a shallow container, large enough to hold the chicken pieces in a single layer, or in an unpunctured plastic bag. Stir in the yoghurt to make a paste. Add the chicken pieces, turning to make sure all are well coated with the spice mixture. (For best flavour, slash skinned thighs in several places before coating with marinade.)

Cover the container and allow to stand for 1–2 hours or refrigerate overnight if possible.

Barbecue on a rack, for 10–20 minutes per side, depending on the thickness of the chicken used. The chicken is cooked when the juices run clear, not pink, when the pieces are pierced. Serves 4.

Barbecued Chicken Breasts

Apricot Glazed Chicken Breasts

This is one of my standbys when I want a quick and easy recipe for dinner guests.

Even when the weather is less than perfect, I barbecue the skinless, boneless breasts, and bring them inside to serve at the table.

 4 skinless, boneless chicken breasts
 1 large clove garlic, crushed
 4 teaspoons light soy sauce
 1 tablespoon olive or other oil
 2 tablespoons apricot jam
 2 teaspoons Dijon mustard
 1 tablespoon orange juice

Put the skinless, boneless breasts in a heavy, unpunctured plastic bag with the crushed garlic, half the soy sauce and the oil. Turn to coat all sides with marinade and leave at least 10 minutes, but preferably longer.

Barbecue on a rack over a moderate heat, turning after 4 minutes. When second side has cooked for 4 minutes, test to see if flesh is cooked to the deepest part by piercing it deeply with a sharp knife. If it is cooked, no pink liquid will appear. Keep cooking until this stage is reached, then brush both sides with a glaze made by heating together (in the kitchen or a small metal container on the barbecue) the remaining soy sauce, the apricot jam, mustard and orange juice. Serve as soon as glaze has browned attractively on both sides. Serves 4.

Variation: If you find it hard to tell when the chicken breast is cooked, cut it in half crosswise, with a very sharp knife, and barbecue, cut sides down, until this surface is cooked.

Barbecued Chicken Breasts

These chicken breasts are good alone, with apricot sauce, or with a little sun-dried tomato paste.

 2 skinless, boneless chicken breasts
 1 tablespoon olive oil
 1 tablespoon light soy sauce
 1 tablespoon Thai sweet chilli sauce

Pound the chicken breasts between two sheets of cling film until they are flattened enough to be evenly thick.

Combine the oil, soy sauce and chilli sauce and brush over both sides of the flattened chicken.

Barbecue on a rack for about 5 minutes per side or until cooked through.

Serve as they are, or with home-made Spiced Apricot Sauce (see page 78) or sun-dried tomato paste. Serves 2.

Apricot Glazed Chicken Breasts

Brilliant Barbecued Beef

What could be more appetising than a juicy steak or a deliciously seasoned hamburger sizzling on your barbecue? To many people, these are the first foods that come to mind when barbecues are mentioned!

You don't have to spend a small fortune when you go shopping for beef to barbecue. Inexpensive cuts of beef can be transformed into tasty treats when you make good use of marinades, sauces and seasonings. And if you add interesting accompaniments and garnishes to carefully seasoned hamburgers, you can serve them to anybody with pride!

Make the most of beef you barbecue by cooking it carefully. To ensure you finish up with juicy, flavourful beef, take care not to overcook it. Since barbecue cooking conditions vary, you need to use good judgment rather than a stop watch when deciding how much cooking is enough!

Quick Beef Satay

Make these kebabs with sirloin or rump steak.

750 g tender steak
1 teaspoon ground cumin
1 teaspoon ground coriander
2 tablespoons dark or light soy sauce
2 tablespoons lemon juice
2 tablespoons oil
2 cloves garlic, crushed
¼ teaspoon chilli powder, approximately

Peanut Sauce:
¼ cup peanut butter
½ cup water
2 tablespoons soft brown sugar
1 tablespoon lemon juice
1 tablespoon dark soy sauce

Cut steak into 2 cm cubes and mix with other ingredients in a plastic bag. Refrigerate for 12–24 hours.

Thread steak onto 12 bamboo skewers, which have been soaked in water, then barbecue on an oiled grill rack over a high heat for about 4 minutes per side.

Stir remaining marinade into peanut sauce ingredients and bring to the boil, thinning with more water if necessary. Brush kebabs with peanut sauce during second half of cooking.

Serve extra sauce with skewered beef. Serves 4.

Peanutty Beefstrips

Carefully cooked, beef schnitzels make economical barbecue fare.

400 g thinly sliced beef schnitzels
1 onion, quartered
2 cloves garlic
2 teaspoons grated root ginger
1 teaspoon freshly ground coriander
2 tablespoons lemon juice
2 teaspoons dark soy sauce
¼ cup brown sugar
¼ cup peanut butter

Slice beef into 1 cm-wide strips, as long as possible. Thread strips onto bamboo skewers in concertina fashion.

Combine remaining ingredients in a food processor. Process until smooth. Add water to thin to the consistency of thick cream if necessary.

Stand skewers, meat-ends down, in a small bowl. Pour marinade over them. Leave to stand for 15–30 minutes.

Drain well, then barbecue close to heat until meat loses its pinkness. Take care not to overcook or meat will toughen.

Heat remaining marinade until boiling. Serve as a dipping sauce with meat. Serves 3–4.

Quick Beef Satay

Home-made Hamburgers

A good hamburger is delicious. Experiment with seasonings, cooking times and cooking methods until you arrive at your perfect personal formula. Unless you like your hamburger patty rare (red in the middle), don't leave out the breadcrumbs because they keep a longer-cooked hamburger moist and juicy. Vary hamburger seasonings as you would the flavours you add to roasts, stews and casseroles. Use combinations to characterise the cooking of different countries and complement them by choosing the appropriate glazes and garnishes.

Serve interesting and unusual combinations of raw or cooked vegetables and fruit with hamburger patties, whether they are served in buns, or without bread. Many steak accompaniments and sauces are just as delicious with hamburgers.

Streamline your production line, especially if you are feeding children. If you make more hamburgers than you need and then freeze them individually, you'll have a 'fast food' bar in your own kitchen.

Hamburger patties thaw fast or they may be cooked from frozen when necessary. If you feel you are competing with fast-food outlets for your children's custom, make sure you have the 'trimmings' they want.

Hamburger Patties

500 g minced beef or lamb
1 slice stale bread, crumbled
2 spring onions, chopped, or 1–2 teaspoons onion juice)
1 teaspoon instant beef stock or
  ½ teaspoon salt
1 teaspoon Worcestershire sauce
1 teaspoon chopped fresh herbs (optional)
½ teaspoon garlic salt
¼ cup milk, approximately

Combine all ingredients except for the milk. Mix lightly but thoroughly, then add milk and mix again until mixture is moist enough to form into patties without cracked edges. Shape into large patties if serving one per person in a hamburger bun, or into small patties if serving two per person on a plate with vegetables or salad.

Barbecue in a wire basket about 20 cm from the heat, turning when browned, or barbecue on a preheated, lightly oiled barbecue plate. Makes 4–8 patties.

Variations

• Add ½–1 cup grated cheddar, or 2 tablespoons parmesan, or 2–4 tablespoons crumbled blue vein cheese to basic mixture, instead of using the instant stock or salt.

• Replace garlic salt and milk with 2 tablespoons finely chopped relish, tomato sauce, or your favourite salsa.

• Replace Worcestershire sauce with grated horseradish.

• Replace Worcestershire sauce with your favourite mixed mustard.

• Leave out herbs and replace Worcestershire sauce with dark soy sauce

• Add ½ teaspoon sesame oil or 1 tablespoon toasted sesame seeds.

• Press cracked peppercorns into large hamburgers before cooking.

Hamburger Toppings
• Sliced tomato with basil-flavoured oil and vinegar dressing

• Sliced radishes, bean or alfalfa sprouts, and cucumber in a slightly sweetened vinegar mixture

• Chopped red and green capsicums (raw or skinned and roasted) with oil and vinegar, hot pepper sauce, and oreganum

• Lightly sautéed or raw mushrooms with mustard and sour cream mixed to a sauce; or, more elegantly, with bearnaise sauce

• Sliced gherkins or dill pickles with fresh dill or spring onions or sour cream

• Sliced onions of different colours and types, crisped by first soaking in cold water

• Grilled cheese and pineapple with gherkin or preserved cherry garnish

• Sauerkraut, mild mustard and/or sour cream with caraway seeds

• Sliced cucumber with a yoghurt, mint and garlic sauce

• Sliced or mashed seasoned avocado with sour cream and sliced tomato.

Hamburger Glazes and Sauces

Patties look and taste better if their outer surfaces are glazed. Mixtures which contain sugar in any form should be added close to the end of cooking time or they will burn before the patty is cooked.

• Use tomato or barbecue sauce, soy sauce, teriyaki sauce, or Worcestershire sauce (plain or heated with a little butter or oil).

• Mixed equal parts of honey, soy sauce and lemon juice, thin apricot or plum jam, or tart jelly, with lemon or orange juice and a little Worcestershire or soy sauce if desired.

Bonza Budget Burgers

This recipe makes eight generous, but economical, burgers which are good served in hamburger buns with plenty of lettuce, relish, etc.

    1 egg
    1 tablespoon Worcestershire sauce
    1 teaspoon curry powder
    1 onion
    1 apple
    1 medium-sized potato
    300 g sausagemeat
    300 g beef mince
    oil for cooking

Assemble all ingredients before you start mixing since apple and potato may brown if left to stand too long before mixing and cooking.

Break the egg into a bowl. Add Worcestershire sauce and curry powder. Grate into the bowl the onion, unpeeled apple and scrubbed potato (skin and all). Stir to coat with egg mixture. Add the sausagemeat and mince, mixing well. With wet hands, divide mixture into 8–10 patties (the patties will be soft, but they will firm up when cooked).

Barbecue on a solid plate, brushed with oil before the burgers are put on it. Cook over a moderate rather than high heat, allowing at least 5 minutes per side. Brown pineapple rings on the hot barbecue plate alongside the burgers if desired.

Serve on toasted halved hamburger buns with your favourite hamburger accompaniments. Makes 8 large burgers.

Variation: Use a food processor to chop the vegetables and apple, then add the meat, using the metal chopping blade.

Above: Bonza Budget Burgers
Below: Hamburger Patties

Thai Beef Salad

To get the right flavour and texture in this dish, the sauce should coat thin slices of rather rare rump steak that has been barbecued in a thick slice and left to stand for about 5 minutes before being sliced. Try this sauce also on moist, skinned barbecued chicken, and on lean lamb rumps, topsides or thick flanks which have been barbecued, then sliced.

250–300 g rump steak, cut thickly

Dressing:
1–2 cloves garlic, crushed
3 cm lemon grass stalk, approximately
2 tablespoons sugar
1 tablespoon fish sauce
2 tablespoons fresh lime juice
2 tablespoons water
¼ teaspoon salt
⅛ teaspoon chilli powder or 1 very thinly sliced fresh chilli
2 tablespoons chopped fresh mint
2 tablespoons chopped coriander leaf
1 spring onion, chopped

Salad:
lettuce leaves of different types
chopped spring onions
cucumber slices
coriander leaves
fresh red chillies (optional)

Trim the steak of all visible fat and remove the membrane around the edges or snip the membrane at intervals. (Steak tends to curl if the membrane is not removed or snipped.) Rub the steak with a little dark soy sauce and a little oil, cover, and leave to stand until about 30 minutes before you want to serve it. Bring steak to room temperature before cooking.

Barbecue the steak on a heavy, oiled barbecue plate until nicely browned on both sides, but still pink in the middle. (Take care not to overcook it.) Put the steak on the carving board and leave it to stand for 5–10 minutes before you slice it thinly into strips.

While the meat cooks and stands (or earlier if it suits you), make the dressing by putting the garlic and thinly sliced lemon grass in a food processor or blender and chopping very finely. Add the next six ingredients and process again. Add the mint, coriander and spring onion, and process until roughly chopped. (Taste to check balance of flavours and add more salt or water to get the flavour you like.) Slice the meat thinly, then toss in part of the dressing.

Attractively combine the salad ingredients on each plate, then arrange the marinated meat on top and drizzle the remaining dressing over the leaves and meat. Garnish with a leaf of coriander, thinly sliced spring onions, mint sprigs or a 'flower' made from a fresh red chilli. Serves 2.

Beef Kebabs

Thread colourful, quick-cooking vegetables between cubes of marinated steak to make sure that your family and friends are eating a well-balanced barbecue meal!

400 g rump or blade steak (after trimming)
1–2 cloves garlic, chopped
1 tablespoon dark soy sauce
1 tablespoon Worcestershire sauce
1 tablespoon sherry or white wine or lemon juice
1 teaspoon oil
300–400 g quick-cooking vegetables, cubed (onion, red, green and yellow capsicums, zucchini, mushrooms, tomatoes)

Trim meat, removing any fat and gristle, and cut into 2 cm cubes. Mix in a plastic bag or bowl with the next five ingredients, and leave for 1 hour.

Cut vegetables into 2 cm squares. Remove meat from marinade and coat vegetables with remaining marinade. Thread onto skewers, allowing two skewers per person, alternating meat and vegetables. Barbecue on an oiled grill rack, close to heat for 5–10 minutes until meat is evenly browned. Serves 4.

Left: Thai Beef Salad
Below: Beef Kebabs

Barbecued Flank Skirt

Barbecued Flank Skirt

As long as you like your steak pink in the middle, you should try this recipe, where a relatively inexpensive steak is marinated, barbecued on a heavy barbecue plate, then sliced thinly across the grain to produce strips of juicy, well-flavoured meat. The steak cut used is called thin flank, or flank skirt. Ask for the whole steak – which comes in an oval or leaf shape, more pointed at one end, weighing about 500–600 g, and about 1–2 cm thick.

500–600 g flank skirt
2 tablespoons dark soy sauce
2 tablespoons lemon juice (or wine vinegar)
2 tablespoons oil
2–3 garlic cloves, crushed

Score both flat surfaces of the meat into diamond shapes using a sharp knife. The cuts should be only 2–3 mm deep, but will enable the marinade to penetrate better.

Place the meat in a heavy-duty plastic bag so it lies flat. Add remaining ingredients, squeeze all air from the bag and secure tightly. Marinate at room temperature for at least 2 hours.

Remove steak from marinade and drain. Barbecue on a preheated lightly oiled barbecue plate, allowing 3–4 minutes per side. Take great care not to overcook the meat. To check whether the meat is cooked to the right stage, cut down to the centre (along the grain of the meat) with a sharp knife. Leave the cooked steak to stand in a warm place for 5–10 minutes before cutting it, holding the knife at a 45° angle to the board, into very thin slices across the grain of the meat. Serves 4–6

Barbecued Rump Steak

Although rump steak is not as tender as steaks from the loin, its flavour is excellent. I am prepared to treat the steak very carefully so I can enjoy its flavour without toughening it. A thick slice of rump, marinated, barbecued, then sliced thinly, is one of my favourite meats.

1 x 4 cm-thick rump steak
2 tablespoons dark soy sauce
strip of lemon or lime rind
2 tablespoons lemon or lime juice
1 tablespoon oil
2 cloves garlic, crushed
1 teaspoon honey or brown sugar
hot pepper sauce
1–2 teaspoons grated fresh ginger root
  (optional)

Trim the steak, removing all outer fat. Snip any membrane since it shrinks faster than the meat, and causes it to curl during cooking. Put the steak between two pieces of cling film, or in a plastic bag, and bang it evenly from one side to the other with a rolling pin, then turn it at right angles and bang it again in the same way.

Measure all the remaining ingredients into a heavy-duty unpunctured plastic bag. Add the steak, squeeze out the air, fasten the bag with a rubber band, and leave it in the refrigerator, preferably for 1–2 days, but for at least half an hour, turning it occasionally. An hour before cooking bring to room temperature. Lift from the marinade and drain off all the excess liquid.

Place steak in a grilling basket and position the meat so that its surface is about 8 cm from the heat. Alternatively, cook steak on a solid plate which has been lightly brushed with oil. Cook for about 6 minutes before turning and cooking for 4–6 minutes longer. Press the centre of the meat at intervals. At first it will be spongy, then it will become springier as it cooks. If you cannot judge its state, cut a small slit and look at its colour to judge doneness.

Leave to stand for at least 6 minutes before slicing then, using a very sharp knife, cut in thin diagonal slices across the grain of the meat.

Serve hot, or at room temperature, with mustard, horseradish sauce, and your favourite vegetables or salad. Serves 2.

Barbecued Rump Steak

Festive Beef Fillet

Although it may seem very extravagant to think about barbecuing beef fillets for a dozen or so people, this is not necessarily the case. I have found that small whole frozen beef fillets (weighing about one kilogram each) are sold at intervals by some large supermarkets for very reasonable prices. They can be kept in your freezer for up to three months. Slowly thawed and carefully cooked on a well-regulated barbecue, they may be served as the main part of a festive summer meal. We have enjoyed these fillets served with horseradish sauce, Dijon mustard and a tangy sauce made from fresh plums. For a well-balanced meal, serve generous amounts of the vegetables which are so plentiful and delicious in summer.

Thaw small fillets slowly in the refrigerator. After 4–8 hours trim the meat, carefully cutting away the silvery membrane appearing on one side. This takes a little time but it is worth it since it may shrink as it cooks, and twist the meat into a curved shape. Tie the trimmed fillet into a compact shape, tucking in the narrow end, using firm string or thread. Place the prepared meat in the marinade transfer to an unpunctured plastic bag and refrigerate for 1–2 days.

Marinade:
  2 tablespoons wine vinegar or ¼ cup red
    or white table wine
  2 tablespoons lemon or orange juice
  2 cloves garlic, squashed
  1 tablespoon light soy sauce
  2 tablespoons olive or other oil
  fresh herbs, bruised, or crumbled dried
    herbs, eg fresh citrus-flavoured thyme and
    crushed tarragon

Plum Sauce:
  3–4 sliced fresh plums
  1 tablespoon smooth mixed mustard
  vegetable cooking liquid or wine to thin
  salt and pepper
  sugar to taste

Take the meat from the refrigerator 1 hour before you are going to cook it, and put it on a pre-heated barbecue rack about 15–18 cm from the heat. Cover the meat as it cooks with a domed barbecue lid or with a tent of doubled aluminium foil (covering it like this encloses some hot air and speeds up cooking.) Have the heat high until the meat has browned on all sides. Throw a few sprigs of the herb used to flavour the marinade on the barbecue bricks during the cooking if you like. This gives a smoky, herby flavour.

Do not turn the meat too soon – wait for about 7–8 minutes so that it has heated through. The total cooking time for a fillet weighing about one kilogram is likely to be about 20 minutes. Turn down the heat when the meat has browned evenly until it has cooked to the stage you like it. (With experience, you can judge when the meat is cooked by pressing it – it should start to feel springy instead of spongy.) Alternatively, make a cut in the thickest part and look at its colour or pierce it and look at the colour of the juices. They should be pink but not bloody.

Leave the meat to stand for 5–10 minutes before carving into diagonal slices. If desired, make the Plum Sauce by simmering sliced plums in the remaining marinade, add the mixed mustard, thin it with vegetable cooking liquid or wine. Strain sauce through a sieve and season carefully to taste, adding a little sugar to bring out the flavours. Serves 6–8.

Handy Hint

If you are using a not-so-tender steak, and have little marinating time, tenderise the steak with a meat hammer as well as using one of the marinades on page 75.

After marinading, pat steak dry, oil its surface lightly, then brown on both sides on a thoroughly preheated plate (or in a heavy pan on the barbecue). If necessary, lower heat to cook until the centre is as you like it.

Festive Beef Fillet

Luscious Lamb Barbecues

For thousands and thousands of years the delicious smell of herb-flavoured lamb cooking over an open fire has been wafting through the Mediterranean countryside.

Using your barbecue, you can quickly and easily achieve much the same results with chops cut from the shoulder, ribs, or middle loin as well as other cuts of lamb.

Rib and middle loin chops are more tender than shoulder chops, and may be cooked without marinating if desired, but they have an excellent flavour if brushed with the lamb marinade of your choice before cooking. Shoulder chops, along with cubes of lamb, are best marinated for a few hours before cooking or, if time is short, left to stand in a marinade at room temperature for at least an hour.

Rib chops and cutlets

Cut away nearly all outer fat. Cut off knobbly bone with pruners or cutting pliers if desired (this bone will probably already be removed from cutlets).

Middle loin chops

Trim as much outer fat and other fat as possible without detaching the tail of the chop. In order that tail meat does not overcook roll it up, towards the small eye of very tender meat, and secure with a toothpick.

Noisettes

Trim fat from middle loin chops as above, then cut around T-shaped bone and remove it. Wind tail around both eyes of meat, and push a bamboo skewer through the rolled chop, from one side to the other. Cut off the skewer, and push the halved remaining skewer at right angles to the other. The crossed skewers will keep the roll of lamb flat and in place as it cooks.

Barbecued Chops

Shoulder chops

Cut off all outer fat, and any bones which are near the edge of the chop. Snip edges to prevent curling during cooking. Bang chops a few times on both sides with a meat hammer if desired. Turn in marinade of choice and leave to stand at room temperature for one hour or up to 24 hours in the refrigerator.

Lamb kebabs

Cubes of lean lamb, 2–3 cm in size, cut from any part of the lamb make good kebabs when they are threaded on bamboo or metal skewers. The cheapest and most juicy are cubes cut from a boned forequarter or shoulder, or from shoulder chops. Although they may be cooked without marinating, they become tenderised if left to stand in your favourite marinade for at least an hour. Do not choose a marinade that has a high sugar content: such a mixture is best brushed on during the last few minutes of cooking to avoid burning. Brush with oil or an oil mixture before barbecuing if meat is very lean.

Lamb racks

A lamb rack is cut from the front end of the loin. It consists of 6–8 rib chops in one piece, and is carefully trimmed. A chined Frenched lamb rack with all its surface fat removed cooks on a barbecue in about 10 minutes and makes a gourmet meal for two. When a rack is chined by a butcher, all the bones except the curved pieces of rib bone are removed so it is easy to carve between each chop. Because the sections of backbone are removed, the tender eye of rib meat cooks evenly. A rack is so tender that it does not need to be marinated, but it can be brushed with any of the lamb marinades in this chapter for extra flavour if desired. Or you can heat a mixture of equal parts of honey, lemon juice, and very finely chopped mint, and brush over the lamb rack during the last few minutes of cooking. Spoon remaining mixture over the carved chops.

Hawaiian Lamb Cutlets

This simple marinade gives lean lamb cutlets an excellent flavour.

    8 lamb cutlets
    1 tablespoon lime or lemon juice
    1 tablespoon sesame oil
    1 tablespoon light soy sauce
    1 clove garlic, crushed

Trim cutlets if necessary, removing all visible fat and any knobbly pieces of bone, then flatten between 2 sheets of cling film, beating them with a rolling pin.

Combine remaining ingredients in a shallow dish and turn the chops in this marinade, leaving them to stand for at least 5 minutes, but preferably longer before cooking.

Barbecue cutlets on a rack close to the heat until meat loses its pink colour. Brush with extra marinade during the cooking time for extra flavour. Serve immediately. Serves 4.

Variation: Use middle loin chops instead of the cutlets – trim and flatten the same way before marinating.

Barbecued Shoulder Chops

Shoulder chops make inexpensive barbecues. For maximum tenderness bang them on both sides with a meat hammer, then turn in a mixture of equal parts of lemon juice, oil and light soy sauce, and leave them to stand for at least 30 minutes, or up to 24 hours in the refrigerator. Brush Barbecue Sauce on chops during the last few minutes of cooking – any sooner and the outside will brown and burn before the centre is cooked.

Barbecue Sauce
    ½ cup tomato sauce
    2 tablespoons soya oil
    1 tablespoon brown sugar
    1 tablespoon Worcestershire sauce
    1 teaspoon dry mustard
    1 teaspoon basil
    1 teaspoon marjoram

Mix all ingredients for the Barbecue Sauce together in a small pan. Bring to the boil then put aside until required. Barbecue the drained, marinated shoulder chops about 5 cm from heat, brushing with Barbecue Sauce when almost cooked.

Indonesian Barbecued Lamb

Lamb is given a very interesting flavour when it is left to stand in this tasty marinade.

    600–700 g lean cubed shoulder lamb
    2 garlic cloves, chopped
    2 teaspoons grated root ginger
    1 teaspoon freshly ground coriander
      seed (optional)
    2 tablespoons dark soy sauce
    2 tablespoons lemon juice
    2 tablespoons oil
    3–4 drops hot pepper sauce
    ¼ cup brown sugar
    3 tablespoons peanut butter
    ¼ cup water

Cut lamb into cubes, trimming away excess fat. Place lamb cubes in an unpunctured plastic bag.

Combine remaining ingredients, preferably in a food processor bowl. Mix to blend. Pour 2 tablespoons of the mixture over the cubed lamb and knead bag to mix. Close bag, leaving lamb to marinate for at least 15 minutes before threading on soaked bamboo or metal skewers.

Heat remaining marinade until smooth and thick, adding a little more lemon juice or water if it is thicker than thin cream.

Barbecue lamb on a rack close to the heat. Brush with marinade when lamb is nearly cooked. Cooked lamb should be pink inside and slightly crusty outside.

Serve with rice or crusty bread rolls, and with a cucumber or mixed green salad. Serves 4.

Barbecued 'Butterflied' Leg of Lamb

The meat from a butterflied leg of lamb is delicious and, as the leg is made up of larger muscles than the forequarter, the slices are bigger than the slices from a boned shoulder. Use Tex-Mex or Mediterranean Marinade, and leave the boned leg to marinate for 24–48 hours before barbecuing on a rack over moderate heat. In cool weather use a domed lid or make an aluminium foil tent to partially cover the meat. The cooking time should be about 30–40 minutes (under good conditions) as the meat is fairly thick. Cook, skin side up, for about 20 minutes, then turn and cook with the skin side down until the meat is cooked to your liking.

Skewered Lamb Fillets

Although lamb fillets cost more than other lamb cuts, they are always very lean and tender and may be cut in pieces and threaded on skewers with very little time and effort.

250–300 g lamb fillets
2 tablespoons lemon juice
1 tablespoon honey
1 tablespoon oil
1 clove garlic, finely chopped

Soak four bamboo skewers in water. Cut the meat into 2 cm slices, trimming off any fat. Put the cubes in an unpunctured plastic bag.

Prepare the marinade by heating remaining ingredients in the microwave on High (100% power) for 20 seconds. Or heat in a small saucepan until the honey has melted. Stir well and cool to room temperature, then pour over the bagged meat and leave to stand while you prepare chosen accompaniments.

Thread the marinated lamb onto the soaked skewers. Cook on a barbecue rack over a high heat for a short time. The kebabs are ready when the outside is brown, and the inside pink but not red. Serves 2.

Note: For a very quick, easy meal, serve two kebabs per person with an avocado half, or with sliced avocado and salsa and your favourite bread (sourdough has a delicious complementary flavour). Salsas to try with this recipe are Kiwifruit Salsa or Fruit Salsa (see page 77).

Glazed Stuffed Noisettes

What better way to celebrate the start of the barbecue season than with glazed noisettes made from succulent young lamb chops.

  8 middle loin lamb chops
  8 thin slices side bacon
  juice of 2 lemons
  ¼ cup redcurrant or cranberry jelly
  2 teaspoons mustard

Cut T-bones from the chops and trim if necessary. Cut the bacon rashers so they are as wide as the chops are thick. Roll the tails of the chops around the 'eyes' of muscle. Wrap the bacon strips around the noisettes. Secure the bacon and keep chops flat by pushing two bamboo skewers or two half skewers at right angles through the meat. Sprinkle with a little of the lemon juice and refrigerate until required.

Barbecue or grill chops for about 5 minutes each side, about 10 cm from the heat.

Heat the remaining lemon juice with the jelly and mustard and brush over the noisettes during the last 2–3 minutes of cooking. Serves 4.

Note: For fillings use interesting and colourful ingredients and combinations, eg cooked peach pieces, strips of red capsicum and wedges of kiwifruit, sautéed mushroom and water chestnut.

East Meets West Noisettes

Noisettes that are left plain or wrapped in a strip of streaky bacon before skewering and barbecuing are delicious with this lemony sauce – the same type of sauce that is sometimes served with chicken in Asian recipes.

Lemon Sesame Sauce:
  ¼ cup sugar
  2 tablespoons cornflour
  1 lemon, grated rind and juice
  1 tablespoon corn or soya oil
  2 tablespoons mild vinegar
  ½ teaspoon sesame oil
  1 cup water

Mix the sugar and cornflour together in a small saucepan. Add remaining ingredients and bring to the boil, stirring constantly. Thin with extra water if necessary. Pour over barbecued noisettes from which the skewers or toothpicks have been removed. Makes enough for 8 noisettes.

Glazed Stuffed Noisettes

Tangy Lamb Noisettes

Noisettes with a fruity filling and a tangy glaze taste very good indeed!

8 middle loin chops
¼ cup orange juice
8 dried apricots
8 prunes
8 rashers side bacon
2 tablespoons light soy sauce

Glaze:
2 tablespoons marmalade
2 tablespoons whisky
2 tablespoons red or white wine vinegar
1 teaspoon finely chopped fresh tarragon or
   thyme, or 1 tablespoon finely chopped mint

Cut away the T-bone and outer fat with a sharp knife. Heat the orange juice and dried apricots until juice boils, then leave to cool.

Enclose an orange juice-soaked dried apricot and prune inside each chop before wrapping the tail around the large and small eyes of meat to make a compact circle.

Wrap a thin strip of side bacon around each noisette. Use the long, thin part of the bacon rasher and cut off the rest to use for something else. Push a bamboo skewer right through the middle of the noisette, from one side to the other, through the filling and the lamb. Cut off the protruding point of the skewer, then push it through the noisette again, at right-angles to the other piece (this stops the centres from popping up during cooking). Brush with light soy sauce, cover and leave to stand until required.

To make glaze, bring all ingredients o the boil and simmer until syrupy.

Barbecue noisettes for 3–4 minutes per side, brushing with the prepared glaze when the meat is nearly cooked. Leave to stand in a warm place for about 5 minutes, then pull out the skewers before serving. Spoon remaining glaze over the noisettes when serving, and garnish with a little of the herb used in the glaze. Serves 4.

Glazed Butterflied Leg of Lamb

Trimmed, marinated, barbecued, and glazed just before serving, this boned-and-opened flat lamb cooks in half an hour!

1 boned leg of lamb
¼ cup white wine or lemon juice
1 tablespoon Worcestershire sauce
1 tablespoon oil
fresh or dried herbs (optional)
½ cup marmalade
2 tablespoons mixed mustard
1 tablespoon dark soy sauce
½ teaspoon hot pepper sauce

Trim outer fat and skin from boned leg of lamb. Cut between the muscles at the thinnest (inner) part of the leg, opening it out flat. Remove fat from the inner surface. Place lamb in an unpunctured plastic bag with the wine or lemon juice, Worcestershire sauce and oil. Add herbs. Squeeze air from bag, fasten with a rubber band and refrigerate overnight.

Barbecue lamb over a moderate heat, covering with a domed lid or with a tent of aluminium foil if the weather is cool, allowing 15–20 minutes per side, depending on size of lamb and intensity of heat. While lamb cooks, heat marmalade with remaining ingredients. Brush over meat during last 5–10 minutes of cooking. Serve extra glaze as a sauce with lamb.

Note: It is important to have the lamb far enough from the heat, or at a low enough heat, to cook the thicker parts without burning the outside. If you feel that the lamb is not cooking evenly enough, slash the thicker muscles on the side closest to the bone.

Marinated Orange Lamb Leg Steaks

Especially good for an easy barbecue in the back garden or on a picnic table in a park. Marinate the leg steaks before you leave home, and carry the tabbouleh in one plastic bag or bowl, and the lettuce leaves in another. Take pita bread to warm on the barbecue alongside the lamb.

8 small lamb leg steaks (500–600 g), sliced
   about 15 mm thick from lamb flank,
   topside, chump (or rump) or silverside
1 tablespoon olive oil
2 tablespoons light soy sauce
3 tablespoons orange juice
2 teaspoons grated orange rind
2 cloves garlic, crushed

Trim off any visible fat and snip edges of the steaks. Put them between two layers of cling film and bang with a rolling pin or meat hammer until meat is about half its original thickness.

Mix the remaining ingredients and brush over both sides of the lamb, or turn the lamb in the mixture in a shallow container. Leave to stand at least 5 minutes, but preferably for several hours in the refrigerator or a cool place.

Preheat the barbecue. Cook lamb on a rack or hot barbecue plate close to the heat, until done to your liking (remembering that lean, trimmed, beaten-out meat is likely to cook in only a few minutes over a moderate heat). Serve with Tabbouleh (see page 65). Serves 4.

Left: Glazed Butterflied Leg of Lamb
Below: Marinated Orange Leg Lamb Steaks

Fruited Lamb Kebabs

If you like roast lamb with apricot stuffing, you should try these barbecued cubes of lamb, skewered with vegetables and dried apricots, and flavoured with rosemary.

    500 g lean boneless lamb
    1 onion
    1 red capsicum
    18–24 good quality dried apricots

Orange Rosemary Sauce:
    1 teaspoon grated orange rind
    ½ cup orange juice
    ¼ cup olive oil
    2 tablespoons white wine vinegar
    1 tablespoon light soy sauce
    2 tablespoons grated raw onion
    1 clove garlic, finely chopped
    2–3 teaspoons very finely chopped
       fresh rosemary.

Trim any fat off the lamb if necessary and cut into 3 cm cubes. Combine ingredients for Orange Rosemary Sauce in a screw-top jar and mix well. Put half aside. Marinate lamb cubes in the rest of the sauce for 30 minutes.

Cut the onion and capsicum into 3 cm squares. Toss with a little of the reserved Orange Rosemary Sauce.

Divide the pieces of marinated lamb, onion, capsicum and apricots into piles to represent the number of kebabs you plan to serve. Thread the lamb cubes, onion, capsicum and apricots alternately onto bamboo skewers. Another option is to thread them onto lengths of rosemary stem that have been stripped of leaves, apart from a few at one end.

Barbecue kebabs, turning frequently and brushing with the remaining marinade at intervals until lamb is cooked to your liking. Do not over-cook. Serves 4.

Above: Fruited Lamb Kebabs
Below: Minted Lamb Mini-Roast

Barbecued Lamb Mini Roasts

A new, exciting butchery idea is to have a leg of lamb or hogget 'seam-boned' so that you get four neat, compact cuts from each leg. These have no fatty outer layer, and are wonderful for small families. The cuts are:

Lamb Rump or Chump
Lamb Topside
Lamb Silverside
Lamb Thick Flank

All can be barbecued very successfully. I sometimes seam-bone a leg of hogget myself, 'butterfly' (or cut open and lie flat) the chunky thick flank and topside muscles, marinate them all, and barbecue the four pieces. Depending on size, appetites and the amount of other food served, each mini-roast will feed 2–4 people. They are easy and neat to carve.

Use the Tex-Mex, Mediterranean or Sesame Marinade (see pages 36–37).

Minted Lamb Mini-Roast

This is one of the ways I cook lamb topside or silverside.

1 lamb mini roast, topside or silverside

Marinade:
¼ cup finely chopped fresh mint
1 clove garlic, finely chopped
2 tablespoons wine vinegar
1 tablespoon olive or other oil

Mix the marinade ingredients in a heavy-duty unpunctured plastic bag. Put the lamb in the bag with the marinade, squeeze out all the air, and leave to stand.

For best flavour and tenderness, leave the lamb in the marinade for 2 hours or longer, otherwise for at least 15 minutes.

Cook lamb on a preheated barbecue, covered with a domed lid or aluminium foil tent if the weather is cool, for 8–10 minutes per side depending on the stage of 'doneness' you like.

To intensify the mint flavour, mix 1–2 teaspoons honey with the leftover marinade, and brush it over the meat several times during the last 5 minutes of cooking.

Remove from the barbecue and leave in a warm place to stand for 10 minutes before carving in slices across the grain of the meat. Slice the meat diagonally for bigger slices. Serves 2–4.

Barbecued Lamb Forequarter

If you like to carve and eat slices of lean lamb that are nicely browned and full of flavour on the outside and pink, tender and succulent in the centre, try barbecuing an inexpensive boned lamb forequarter from your supermarket. For maximum tenderness, prepare the meat and put it in its marinade in the refrigerator one or even two days before you plan to cook it. Left-overs are good cold.

1 lamb or hogget forequarter, boned and rolled
Tex-Mex Marinade or Mediterranean
    Marinade (see pages 36–37)

Remove the net, string or skewers holding the boned shoulder together and unroll the meat, skin side down. Using a sharp knife, cut away any visible fat and membrane between the muscles, and cut any large chunky muscles so that the whole forequarter lies flat. Turn the meat over so that the skin side is up, and trim away as much fat as you can without the meat falling apart.

Put trimmed meat in an unpunctured plastic bag with the chosen marinade ingredients, and gently knead to massage the marinade into the meat, working from outside the bag. Squeeze all air from the bag, fasten with a rubber band, and refrigerate for 12–48 hours. About 4 hours before the meat is to be barbecued, bring back to room temperature.

Place the meat, skin side up, on the preheated oiled grilling rack of the barbecue. Cover with a domed lid or with a tent made from a doubled piece of aluminium foil (this traps heated air so the upper surface of the meat is kept warm while the lower surface cooks). When all the lower surfaces are nicely browned, after about 10–15 minutes, turn the lamb over and cook the other side. In good conditions the lamb will cook in 20–30 minutes. The meat should feel springy, not spongy, when cooked. If in doubt, cut a thick part with a sharp knife and see if the centre is done to the stage that you like it. Cook for longer if necessary. Leave to stand, covered for 10–15 minutes, then carve in slices across the grain of the meat. Serves 6.

Barbecued Leg Lamb Steaks

Lamb Marinades

These marinades taste good on chops, noisettes, kebabs and other lamb cuts. They keep the meat fresh, add interesting flavours to the lamb as it cooks, and make the meat more tender, too – as long as the marinade surrounds the meat for some time.

When lamb is put in a marinade for 30 minutes or less, it may be left at room temperature. For longer marinating, however, the meat should be refrigerated. All marinade recipes make enough for 1 kg of lamb.

Tex-Mex Marinade

1 tablespoon ground cumin
2 teaspoons oreganum
½–1 teaspoon chilli powder
juice of 2–3 lemons
2 tablespoons Worcestershire sauce
2 tablespoons oil
2–3 cloves garlic, crushed

Combine all ingredients in a covered jar or in a food processor.

Barbecued Lamb Leg Steaks

These days I buy a whole leg of lamb and separate the individual muscles, using my thumb and a sharp knife, or I ask my butcher to 'seam out' the leg for me.

Whether I do it myself, or the butcher does it for me, I finish up with two chunky cuts: the thick flank and the topside; and two flatter cuts: the chump or rump, and the silverside. These four compact cuts can be wrapped and refrigerated or frozen, then used as required – roasted, barbecued whole, or cut into steaks, cubes (for kebabs) or schnitzels. The topside and thick flank make nice round steaks.

The meat is so tender it does not really need marinating, but it tastes especially good if the steaks have stood for a few minutes in a mixture of equal amounts of soy sauce, sherry and lemon juice and oil, flavoured with a little chopped garlic. I snip the edges of the steaks to prevent them curling, then cook them on a hot barbecue plate, or on the rack of my barbecue. Serve leg steaks with your favourite fruit salsa (see page 77) and with halved or sliced avocado.

East-West Marinade

2 tablespoons dark or light soy sauce
2 tablespoons lemon juice
1 tablespoon honey
2 cloves garlic, crushed
2 teaspoons sesame oil (optional)

Combine all ingredients in a covered jar.

Sesame Marinade

¼ cup light soy sauce
¼ cup lemon juice
2 tablespoons sesame oil
½–1 teaspoon hot pepper sauce
2 garlic cloves, crushed

Leave lamb in marinade for at least 24 hours. Barbecue over a high heat on the grilling rack, preferably covered with a domed lid or aluminium foil tent, for 8–12 minutes per side, depending on the conditions and the stage to which you like the meat cooked.

Oriental Marinade

2 tablespoons lemon juice
2 tablespoons dark soy sauce
1 tablespoon brown sugar
1 tablespoon oil
1 clove garlic, crushed
1 teaspoon root ginger (optional)

Combine all ingredients in a covered jar.

Mediterranean Marinade (1)

1 tablespoon chopped rosemary leaves or
   2 teaspoons fresh thyme leaves
2 teaspoons dried oreganum
juice of 2–3 lemons
2 tablespoons Worcestershire sauce
2 tablespoons oil
3 cloves garlic, crushed

Combine all ingredients in a covered jar or in a food processor.

Mediterranean Marinade (2)

¼ cup red or white wine or 2 tablespoons
   wine vinegar
2 tablespoons olive or other oil
1 teaspoon dried basil
1 teaspoon dried oreganum
¼ teaspoon dried thyme, optional
1 tablespoon Worcestershire sauce (optional)

Combine all ingredients in a covered jar.

Yoghurt Marinade

¼ cup plain yoghurt
2 teaspoon honey (optional)
2 tablespoons chopped fresh mint
½–1 teaspoon ground cumin
½–1 teaspoon ground coriander
½–1 teaspoon paprika (optional)

Combine all ingredients in a covered jar.

Lamb Glazes

Sweet mixtures brushed over barbecued lamb near the end of the cooking time give a shiny appearance and an interesting flavour. However, if a glaze is added too soon, the sugar in it will burn before the lamb is cooked. Some recipes call for heating the glaze ingredients before brushing them over barbecued meat. This reduces the glaze to a thickish, rather syrupy consistency.

Apricot Glaze

2 tablespoons apricot jam
1 tablespoon mixed mustard
2–3 tablespoons orange or lemon juice
1 tablespoon oil

Tomato Glaze

2 tablespoons tomato sauce
1 tablespoon Worcestershire sauce
1 tablespoon brown sugar
1 tablespoon oil

Oriental Glaze

1 tablespoon soy sauce
1 tablespoon brown sugar
1 tablespoon lemon juice
1 tablespoon oil

Mouth-watering Pork and Sausages

Can you think of anything more tempting than sizzling spareribs, straight from the barbecue? Mouth-watering though these may be, don't think that pork barbecues start and finish with these favourite treats. Other cuts of lean pork barbecue well, too. I find that tender pork fillets make really easy and reliable barbecues for friends invited after we have all finished a hard day's work, while kebabs of lean low-fat, pork are the most quickly barbecued meats in my repertoire. And when you have a crowd of hungry children to satisfy, the humble sausage – often stuffed with pork – is more likely to be 'top of the pops' than any other meat. Make the most of interesting 'gourmet sausages' at other times. You can serve these to your most discerning friends with pride, as long as you have cooked them well!

Barbecued Pork Ribs

It's no use planning a slow-cooking pork rib recipe, because people who are addicted to them just can't wait too long! Although this recipe calls for preliminary work in the kitchen, it is worth it.

    1–1.5 kg meaty pork rib bones
    1 cup water
    1 teaspoon cumin

Sauce:
    1 onion
    2 cloves garlic
    1 tablespoon oil
    1 teaspoon ground cumin
    ½ teaspoon ground coriander seed
    ½ cup tomato sauce
    2 tablespoons Worcestershire sauce
    2 tablespoons soft brown sugar
    1 tablespoon wine or cider vinegar

Barbecued Pork Ribs

    1 tablespoon tomato paste
    ½ teaspoon cornflour
    ½ cup water
    ¼ teaspoon chilli powder

Cut the pork ribs into sections, each with three or four rib bones, and place in a large saucepan with the water and ground cumin. Cover tightly and simmer for 1 ½ hours or until the meat is very tender.

While the pork cooks, make the sauce. Put the first five ingredients into a food processor, chop very finely, transfer to a pan and cook over a moderate heat for about 5 minutes. Measure the remaining ingredients into the pan and simmer for about 15 minutes.

When required, place the rib sections on the barbecue, heat on each side until they sizzle, then brush with the warm sauce, and heat again on both sides. Serve with crusty bread, warmed on the barbecue or with corn cobs. Serves 4.

Handy Hint

You can precook sausages just before you barbecue them or cook them in advance, then refrigerate them. Simmer the sausages gently in a large covered pan, with a little beer or water, until they feel firm, about 20 minutes. Pour away and discard any fatty liquid. For larger numbers of sausages, bake in a covered roasting pan with a little added liquid for about 30 minutes at 150 °C.

To precook sausages in the microwave oven, put them in one layer in an oven bag or covered container, and allow about 15 minutes on Medium (50% power) for 500 g of sausages.

Japanese Pork Fillet

Don't be put off by the large amount of sesame oil in this delicious recipe. The flavour of the pork is wonderful when the exact amounts given in the recipe are used.

400–500 g pork fillet
1 tablespoon grated fresh ginger
1 large clove garlic, finely chopped
2 tablespoons light soy sauce
pinch cayenne pepper
¼ cup sesame oil
3 tablespoons wine vinegar
1 teaspoon cornflour
2 tablespoons water

Trim the pork fillet of any fat and untidy ends if necessary. Put the whole fillet into an unpunctured plastic bag with the next six ingredients. Turn the bag to mix the ingredients well and to coat the pork with the marinade. Marinate for at least 30 minutes, or up to 24 hours (refrigerate the meat in the marinade when using a longer time).

Preheat the barbecue. Remove pork from the bag and reserve the marinade. Cook pork for 4 minutes each side, then leave to stand for about 10 minutes before carving into 1 cm slices. The meat should be cooked enough to lightly brown the outside and to cause the meat inside to turn from pink to light beige, with only a slight rosy glow in the centre. If you are not sure, cut the fillet in two, crosswise, at the end of the cooking time – in the event of any bright pink flesh, cook for a little longer.

Mix the cornflour and water in a small saucepan or microwave jug. Add the reserved marinade and heat until the mixture boils and thickens.

Serve the sliced pork with a salad and a little of the thickened sauce drizzled over. Serves 3–4.

Above: Japanese Pork Fillet
Below: Stuffed Pork Fillet

Stuffed Pork Fillet

This recipe is suitable for use on a barbecue that has a lid to keep the heat in and which will cook at a moderate rather than a very high heat. The pork fillet will dry out if overcooked on the outside before the middle is cooked.

2 pork fillets (200–250 g each)
2 teaspoons mixed mustard
2 tablespoons light soy sauce
1 tablespoon olive oil
2–4 prunes
2–4 dried apricots
¼ cup orange juice
grated rind of ½ orange (optional)
1 tablespoon brandy (optional)
2 tablespoons pine nuts or chopped
   blanched almonds
1–2 teaspoons fresh rosemary and/or sage,
   finely chopped

Open pork fillets flat and brush on both sides with some of the mustard, light soy sauce and oil. Leave to stand for about 15 minutes.

Open prunes flat and quarter the dried apricots. Combine the orange juice and rind, add prunes and apricots and simmer until the fruit is soft. Add brandy, cook for a little longer, then place mixture down the centre of one fillet. Top with pine nuts, add chopped herbs, then cover with the remaining fillet so the wide end of one fillet is over the narrow end of the other. Skewer fillets together with two rows of toothpicks. Brush with remaining mustard, soy and oil mixture.

Stand pork on a barbecue rack on several sprigs of rosemary and/or sage if these are available. Barbecue over a moderate heat under a domed lid, turning after 10 minutes. Test after 20 minutes, cutting fillets in half crosswise if necessary.

When ready, the fillet close to the fruit filling should just have lost its pinkness.

Leave to stand for 10 minutes before removing toothpicks and carving.

Serve with a light fruity chutney. Serves 2.

Peanutty Pork Kebabs

500 g pork steaks
½ cup peanut butter
2 tablespoons light soy sauce
4 tablespoons sherry
1 tablespoon brown sugar
1 clove garlic, finely chopped
2 tablespoons toasted sesame seeds

Cut pork steaks into 2 cm cubes and thread onto bamboo skewers.

Combine the peanut butter, soy sauce, sherry, brown sugar and garlic, mixing until smooth. Refrigerate in a covered container until required (leftover mixture will keep for up to a week). Thin down with a little more sherry or water just before use, then brush evenly over the skewered meat. Sprinkle kebabs on all sides with toasted sesame seeds.

Barbecue kebabs, turning several times, for 5–6 minutes altogether, or until the meat is no longer pink at its thickest part. Test by cutting a cube in half if you are not sure when meat is ready.

Serve immediately. The kebabs will be spoilt if they overcook or are reheated. Serves 4.

Pork Kebabs

Use lean pork steaks to cut into cubes. Leave the cubes of pork to stand in their marinade for at least an hour before grilling them over a high flame on a preheated barbecue.

750 g lean pork steaks

Marinade:
   1 tablespoon dark soy sauce
   1 rounded tablespoon honey
   1 tablespoon sherry
   1 tablespoon sesame oil
   1 teaspoon grated fresh ginger
   ½–1 teaspoon hot pepper sauce
   2 cloves garlic, crushed
   3–4 pineapple rings (optional)
   1 red capsicum (optional)
   1 green capsicum (optional)

Cut the pork into cubes and place them in an unpunctured plastic bag. Measure the marinade ingredients into the bag with the pork and knead gently to mix. Squeeze all the air out of the bag, fasten with a rubber band and leave to stand at room temperature for at least an hour, or in the refrigerator overnight.

Divide the cubes into 12 even groups and thread on 12 soaked bamboo skewers, alone, or with cubes of pineapple and squares of blanched red and green capsicum between the cubes of meat.

Barbecue kebabs over a high heat, turning after 2 minutes. Brush with remaining marinade before and after turning. Kebabs are cooked as soon as pork feels firm, and a cube is no longer pink in the centre. Test after 4 minutes. Take care not to overcook these kebabs or they will be dry. Serves 4.

Pork Fillet Dinner

Pork Fillet Dinner

Pork fillets cook in about 15 minutes on a pre-heated, oiled barbecue plate. Serve corn cobs barbecued in their husks on the barbecue rack at the same time, and warm up bread rolls on the rack for a few minutes.

Overcooked pork fillet is dry and disappointing, so take care to cook it only as much as is necessary.

2 cloves garlic
2 teaspoons olive oil
1 pork fillet (about 400 g)
2 teaspoons balsamic vinegar

Crush garlic and mix with the oil. Rub over all surfaces of the pork fillet.

Barbecue for 10 minutes on a lightly oiled, preheated heavy barbecue plate, turning frequently. When the outside is evenly browned, slice the fillet lengthwise, cutting about three-quarters of the way through. Press the opened cut surface onto the hot plate and cook for about 1 minute longer. This will ensure that the centre cooks.

Sprinkle the vinegar over the meat, turn, then remove from the heat and stand for 5 minutes before carving diagonally into slices.

Serve with Barbecued Corn Cobs (see page 57), Apple, Onion and Tomato Savoury (see page 57), and bread rolls. Serves 2–3.

Barbecued Ham Steaks

Ham steaks are already cooked so just need to be heated through with a glaze to add a little sweetness.

4 ham steaks

Marinade:
¼ cup pineapple juice
1 tablespoon tomato or barbecue sauce
1 teaspoon Dijon mustard
1 teaspoon cornflour
1 teaspoon light soy sauce
1 tablespoon brown sugar

Mix the marinade ingredients together. Heat until boiling, stirring until thick and clear.

Snip the edges of each steak in 4–6 places so steaks will not curl up as they cook. Pour marinade over ham steaks and place in an unpunctured plastic bag or in a shallow dish. Make sure that all ham surfaces are coated. Leave for at least 15 minutes.

Barbecue ham steaks over a high heat on a hot plate or oiled grilling rack until steaks are hot and lightly browned on both sides, about 3–5 minutes per side. Do not overcook.

Barbecue fresh or canned pineapple rings to serve with each steak if desired. Brush pineapple with a mixture made by stirring together, over a low heat, 1 tablespoon each of honey and light soy sauce. Place pineapple on an oiled, heated plate, or in a hinged wire basket, since slices break easily when turned. Serves 4.

Sausages

In all probability, a sausage was the first barbecued food most of us ever tasted!

Well-regulated heat is very important if you want to produce a good barbecued sausage. Nobody wants sausages which are charred on the outside and raw in the middle, yet many barbecued sausages finish up like this. There are several ways of coping with this problem. Start with uncooked sausages of regular thickness, turn the heat to low, and move and rotate the sausages regularly so that they heat through slowly, and the centres cook before the outsides darken too much.

Choose long 'skinny' sausages instead of thicker ones – they cook through faster, requiring half to three-quarters of the cooking time needed by regular sausages.

You can also buy precooked sausages or precook your own before you take them outside to barbecue. In the precooking process, the important thing is to cook the centre of the sausages. The outside will brown well on the barbecue later.

Barbecue your sausages on a solid plate or on a grilling rack – both give good results. For ease in turning a large number of small sausages over a rack, put them in a double-sided wire basket.

Avoid fatty uncooked sausages since they tend to drip and produce a lot of fat which burns and chars the surface of the sausages. Precooked sausages generally produce much less fat as they brown and heat through.

Remember that all sausages were not created equal! There are many types of sausage available these days. Some are unmemorable but inexpensive, and need good sauces, relishes, breads and salads to turn them into an interesting meal, while at the other end of the sausage market are 'designer' sausages that you can serve to anyone with pride.

Handy Hint

All sausages should brown and look attractive without marinades, basting sauces or glazes. If you do want to add glazes, brush them on at the end of the cooking time to prevent over-browning.

Sauces for Sausages

Interesting sauces will make all the difference to plain barbecued or grilled sausages. Serve a selection, with different flavours and textures, so your friends have a choice.

Satay Sauce

½ cup chopped roasted peanuts
2 teaspoons chopped root ginger
1 tablespoon brown sugar
2 cloves garlic
juice of 1 lemon
2 tablespoons light soy sauce
3–4 drops hot pepper sauce
1 cup coconut milk, approximately

Using a food processor or blender, finely chop the first four ingredients together then add the lemon juice, sauces and enough coconut milk to make a thin sauce.

Heat until boiling, thinning more if necessary.

Serve hot. (Can be refrigerated for up to 2–3 days). Serves about 6.

Barbecue Bean Sauce

2 medium-sized onions, chopped
2 cloves garlic, finely chopped
1 tablespoon oil
440 g can baked beans
¼ cup tomato paste
¼ cup brown sugar
2 tablespoons mixed mustard
1 tablespoon Worcestershire sauce
2 tablespoons cider vinegar
water or beer for thinning

Lightly brown onion and garlic in oil in a large pan. Add remaining ingredients and simmer for 10 minutes, stirring often. Thin with water or beer if desired.

Spoon over burgers and barbecued sausages. (Refrigerates well up to 1 week). Makes enough for about 12 servings.

Sage and Apple Sauce

1 onion, chopped
2 tablespoons butter
2 large apples, peeled and sliced
1 tablespoon chopped fresh sage
2 tablespoons apple juice, white wine
  or water
2–3 teaspoons sugar
salt and pepper

Cook the chopped onion in the butter over a moderate heat until golden brown. Add apple, sage, the liquid of your choice, and sugar. Cover and cook until apple is tender. Mash or purée, then season with salt and pepper to taste.

Serve warm or hot with barbecued sausages. (Can be refrigerated for up to 3 days). Serves about 6.

Barbecued Sausages

Succulent Seafood

It's hard to beat a meal of freshly caught fish, lightly cooked to perfection on a barbecue. Because fish is delicate, and cooks quickly, it must be handled carefully if you want good results when you barbecue it.

Double-sided hinged grilling baskets enable fish to be turned easily without breaking up. Flat grilling baskets (the same that you use for hamburgers) are perfect for small whole flatfish, fish steaks and cutlets, and fillets. Fish-shaped grilling baskets are good for whole roundfish. Use them over barbecue racks (grids).

Fish may also be cooked on a solid plate or wrapped in aluminium foil but, while these two methods are useful at times, they do not produce the slightly smoky flavour which fish gets when it is cooked over the coals.

Fish should never be overcooked, since its tender flesh dries up, shrinks and toughens when cooked more than it should be.

If you need convincing of the ease, speed and delicious flavour of barbecued fish, start by barbecuing a small whole flatfish. As long as you do not overcook it, you cannot help but be impressed!

Handy Hint

To barbecue whole roundfish, you may want to invest in a curved, fish-shaped hinged basket which will cradle your fish while it barbecues over the grill rack. The fresh fish should be gutted (from as small a slit as possible) and the body cavity cleaned and filled with herbs, lemon slices, crushed garlic, sliced onion, etc, for extra flavour. Wild fennel leaves, dill leaves, wild marjoram or wild mint from riverbanks add interesting flavours. (Only use herbs you can identify – even though they are not to be eaten, they delicately flavour the flesh.)

Spiced Barbecued Sole or Flounder

Whether you are cooking for your family or a few friends, a small whole flatfish per person, quickly cooked on a barbecue, served with a warmed, crusty bread roll and a cucumber and tomato salad is very tasty, and impressively quick. Since each small flounder cooks in 2–3 minutes in good conditions, it is easy to cook one fish after another, until everyone is served.

Seasoning Mix:
  1 teaspoon chilli powder
  1 teaspoon paprika
  1 teaspoon garlic powder
  1 teaspoon ground cumin
  1 teaspoon salt
  1 teaspoon powdered oreganum

  4 teaspoons oil
  4 teaspoons light soy sauce
  4 teaspoons lemon juice
  4 scaled flatfish, 200–300 g each

Mix the first six ingredients together in a shaker.

Warm together the oil, light soy sauce and lemon juice.

Make 3 or 4 parallel diagonal cuts to the bone on each side of the fish to allow for more even cooking. Brush the oil mixture on each side. Place one or two flatfish in a hinged flat grilling basket for easiest handling and easy turning. Sprinkle each side generously with the seasoning mix, and barbecue over a high heat until the flesh at the thickest part will flake when tested with a fork. This may be as soon as 1 minute for a small fish. Turn and cook the second side.

Serve immediately, with a squeeze of lemon or lime juice, and a little extra seasoning if you like.

Barbecued Salmon Steaks

Salmon steaks have such a lovely flavour of their own that they need few added flavours. I usually cook them outdoors then take them inside to serve more formally!

    4 salmon steaks (100–150 g each)
    25 g butter, melted, approximately
    2 teaspoons light soy sauce
    2 teaspoons lemon or lime juice
    ¼ teaspoon hot pepper sauce, approximately

Pat salmon steaks dry if necessary. Melt butter and stir in the soy sauce, lemon or lime juice and hot pepper sauce. Brush the fish lightly with this mixture, covering all surfaces.

Place steaks in a hinged grilling basket which has been sprayed with non-stick spray or brushed with oil. Brush both sides of the fish with more of the lemon mixture. Cook quite close to a moderately high heat until the salmon loses its translucency and feels firm rather than spongy when you press it and when the flesh flakes when a small fork or sharp knife is twisted in the thickest part. This may happen in as short a time as 1 minute with a fairly thin steak.

Serve immediately, with lemon wedges or with Hollandaise Sauce (see page 76) which has been made ahead and warmed by standing in a container of warm, not hot, water. Serves 4.

Orange Groper Steaks

    2 groper steaks (about 150 g each)
    flour for sprinkling
    1 teaspoon finely grated orange rind
    1 tablespoon orange juice
    1 teaspoon light soy sauce
    ¼ teaspoon very finely chopped garlic
    1 tablespoon melted butter

Pat groper steaks dry if necessary. Sprinkle lightly on both sides with flour.

Thoroughly coat a wire grilling basket with non-stick spray or oil, and place the lightly floured steaks in it.

Combine the next five ingredients in a small pan and brush over both sides of the groper steaks.

Barbecue over a moderate heat, quite close to the heat, for about 2 minutes per side, or until flesh is no longer translucent in the middle when checked with a pointed knife.

Serve immediately with lemon wedges.

Above: Barbecued Salmon Steaks
Below: Orange Groper Steaks

Fisherman's Treat

If you are in the lucky position of catching a number of fish, try this way of cooking them 'on the spot' on your barbecue. Mix the dry seasonings before you leave home, and carry them with you in film canisters!

You will need to alter cooking times to suit the size of your fish. Try any whole sea fish such as kahawai, snapper, tarakihi, gurnard, etc. Gut the fish but scale it only if you want to eat the skin, since you can easily lift off skin and scales after the fish is cooked.

The important thing about cooking fish is not to overdo it. Only a little liquid should form around the fish if it is cooked for the right period of time. It is cooked if the flesh in the thickest part is firm enough to flake when tested with a fork.

1 cleaned fish, skin on (1–1.5 kg)
1 teaspoon celery salt
1 teaspoon garlic salt
1 teaspoon onion salt
1 teaspoon hickory smoke salt
1 teaspoon lemon pepper
1 teaspoon ground cumin
1 teaspoon oreganum
2 lemons
parsley and dill sprigs, if available
1 tablespoon butter, approximately

For even cooking cut several slashes down to the bone on each side of the fish where the flesh is thickest. Sprinkle the mixed dry seasonings both inside the cavity and over the skin. Squeeze one of the lemons and pour the juice over the inside and outside of the fish. Cut the other lemon into slices and place slices evenly along the cavity of the fish, then fill the cavity with sprigs of parsley and dill sprigs if you have them. Dot the butter around, some inside and some outside, the fish.

Wrap the fish carefully in two layers of heavy aluminium foil, sealing the edges carefully so that you can turn the parcel over half way through the cooking time.

Place the package on a barbecue rack over a high heat. Turn every 5 minutes, taking care not to damage the foil. Alternatively, use a fish-shaped wire basket, turning every 5 minutes. The cooking time will vary with the size and shape of the fish. The only way to test is to unwrap the package at intervals and check to see whether the flesh at the thickest part will flake, and if a little liquid has formed around the fish.

Allow the cooked fish to cool for about 10–15 minutes to make handling easier. Pour off, strain and save any juice which is around the fish. Lift away the head, tail and the large and small fins, peel away the skin then lift the flesh from the bones in chunks. Put the flesh on to clean aluminium foil or in a shallow bowl and pour over it any juice. Taste critically. If you feel it is bland, sprinkle the flesh with a little more of the seasonings used in the cooking. Turn the pieces without breaking up further.

Serve the fish at room temperature with Kiwifruit Salsa (see page 77), which can either be served alongside or tossed through the flaked fish. You can also serve mayonnaise with the fish.

Fisherman's Treat

Mustardy Marinated Mussels

These mussels taste delicious after they have stood in their marinade for an hour or longer. You might like to consider opening the mussels on your barbecue after your meal, while the barbecue is still hot, so you can enjoy them the next day.

½ cup sugar
1 tablespoon dry mustard powder
1 teaspoon salt
1 cup wine or cider vinegar

Prepare the sauce ahead, boiling all the ingredients together for 1–2 minutes. Cool and place in a large jar.

Open the mussels over the barbecue as for marinated mussels. Drop the opened, just-cooked mussels into the cool marinade in the jar. Make sure that all the mussels are completely covered with the marinade, then leave to stand for at least an hour before eating.

Refrigerate for up to 3 days if desired.

Marinated Mussels and Mustardy Marinated Mussels

Marinated Mussels

If you can wait, leave these mussels to stand for at least 15 minutes before you eat them!

24–36 fresh uncooked mussels in the shell
½–1 cup liquid from mussels or white wine
1 teaspoon salt
1 teaspoon sugar
¼ cup wine vinegar

Make sure the mussels are alive. They should be tightly closed or should close quickly when tapped with a knife. Place mussels in a flat hinged basket and put on the barbecue rack. Heat, turning *every* 30 seconds, so both sides warm through.

Tilt the hinged basket as the shells open, catching the mussel liquid in a shallow bowl. Open the hinged basket as mussels open further. When shells are completely open and the mussels are plump, remove from shells and put in the bowl with the liquid before they start to shrink and overcook.

If you have not saved much liquid, add enough white wine or water to make liquid up to at least half a cup. Add the salt, sugar and vinegar. Leave to stand for at least 15 minutes or refrigerate for up to 3 days.

Serve on toothpicks or wrapped in fresh buttered bread.

Garlic Mussels

Always popular with lovers of seafood, these make an inexpensive meal.

24–36 fresh uncooked mussels in the shell
50 g butter
3–4 garlic cloves, finely chopped
2 tablespoons lemon juice
4 drops hot pepper sauce
¼ cup chopped parsley (or mixed fresh herbs)

Check that all the mussels you use are tightly closed. Scrub them, pulling away any hairy 'beards'.

Put the butter, garlic, lemon juice and hot pepper sauce in a small metal container and heat over the barbecue until mixture bubbles.

Place mussels on the rack of a barbecue, turning them *every* 30 seconds (so both sides heat) until the shells open. Lift one opened mussel at a time off the barbecue, using tongs. Pour away the liquid from the shell, remove and discard the upper part of the shell if desired, and spoon a little of the butter mixture around the partly cooked mussel. Replace on the barbecue again to warm through. Watch carefully, removing them from the rack before they shrink and toughen.

Serve immediately with buttered bread and lemon wedges. Serves 4–6.

Garlic Mussels

Fresh Fishburgers

Fresh Fishburgers

Don't think of burgers as made only from meat. Fish makes wonderful patties, which are especially good sandwiched between split buns which have been lightly toasted while the fish cooks. These fishburgers may be made from any boneless, skinless fish fillets. Use whatever fresh fish is good value for money.

```
3 slices day-old bread
several sprigs parsley
1 small onion, chopped
500 g boneless, skinless fish fillets
1 egg
1 teaspoon salt
pepper to taste
1 cup milk, approximately
2 tablespoons canola or olive oil
6 hamburger buns or bread rolls
lettuce leaves
sliced tomato
sliced cucumber
```

Break each slice of bread into 4–6 pieces and chop in a food processor fitted with a metal chopping blade. Add the parsley and process until it is chopped finely through the breadcrumbs. Add the chopped onion and process again.

Cut any skin off the fish fillets, remove any bones, then cut into about 2 cm cubes. Add to the breadcrumbs in the processor with the egg

and seasonings. Process in bursts, adding three-quarters of the milk gradually, until the fish is puréed and mixed evenly through the crumbs. The mixture should be moist enough to hold together in patties when shaped with wet hands. Use more or less milk than specified to get them to this stage. (Do not process more than is necessary as the patties will be tough when cooked.)

Brush a little oil on a solid barbecue plate, add the patties and cook over a moderate heat until lightly browned. Turn and cook other side (about 8–10 minutes altogether).

Toast the hamburger buns or bread rolls over the barbecue rack while the fish cooks. Top each bun with lettuce leaves, a cooked fish pattie and some slices of tomato and cucumber. Top with the rest of the toasted bun and serve immediately. Makes 6 burgers.

Tunaburgers

Canned tuna gives these fish patties a mild flavour which is likely to be popular with children.

```
1 cup canned tuna
2 eggs
1 cup fresh breadcrumbs
2 spring onions, chopped
fresh parsley and dill (optional)
salt to taste
4 hamburger buns or bread rolls
```

Drain all the liquid from the tuna and flake it with two forks. Mix the tuna with the unbeaten eggs in a medium-sized mixing bowl with a fork.

Make the breadcrumbs either by using a food processor or by breaking up the bread and rubbing between the palms of your hands. Chop the spring onions and herbs very finely with a sharp knife or add them to the crumbs in the processor. Tip the crumbs into the fish and egg mixture and add salt if necessary. Mix well with a fork, leave to stand for 5 minutes, then add more crumbs if the mixture is too soft, or a little milk if too firm to form into four patties.

Cook the patties in a little oil on a solid barbecue plate, allowing about 5 minutes per side.

Toast the split hamburger buns or bread rolls on the barbecue rack while the burgers cook.

Serve the patties in the toasted buns with carrot and celery sticks alongside. Makes 4 burgers.

Variation: Replace tuna with canned salmon.

Spicy Cajun Fish Fillets

1 tablespoon paprika
¼ teaspoon chilli powder
2 teaspoons ground cumin
1 teaspoon garlic salt
1 teaspoon dried oreganum
1 teaspoon dried thyme
½ teaspoon turmeric
1 tablespoon flour
600 g boneless, skinless tarakihi fillets
olive or other oil

Measure all the seasonings and the flour into a dry jar with an airtight top. Shake well to mix.

Cut each fish fillet into two pieces by continuing the cut made before purchase to remove the central bones, then cut the larger of these pieces diagonally in half. You should finish up with three evenly sized and shaped pieces of fish from each fillet.

Brush each piece of fish lightly with oil of choice, then coat evenly in the seasoning mixture in a shallow plate.

Place the coated fish pieces close together in a hinged grilling basket which has been sprayed with non-stick spray or oil. Cook over a fairly high heat, turning after about 2 minutes, until the flesh in the thickest part is milky when tested with a fork, probably 3–4 minutes.

Serve fish with wedges of fresh lime or lemon, with a stir-fried vegetable mixture over noodles, and garlic bread. Or more simply with crusty bread and a salad. Serves 4.

Foiled Fish

Aluminium foil parcels make excellent containers for small pieces of soft-fleshed fish in an interesting sauce.

750 g boneless fish fillets, cut in pieces
3 tablespoons lemon juice
2 tablespoons light soy or fish sauce
½ teaspoon hot pepper sauce
1 tablespoon chopped coriander leaf or
  spring onion
1 tablespoon oil
2 teaspoons cornflour
1 teaspoon finely chopped garlic (optional)

Combine all ingredients in an unpunctured plastic bag, and knead gently to mix. Refrigerate until required.

Make up four squares of doubled aluminium foil and put quarter of the fish on each. Fold foil over fish and seal edges, rolling foil over

several times to exclude air. Finished packages should be about 10 x 15 cm. Cook over a grill rack for preference or on a hot plate. In good conditions, fish should cook in 2–3 minutes per side. Test one package if necessary. Flesh should be milky white and any liquid slightly thickened.

Serve foil packets on plates so diners can unfold or cut open their own portions. Serve with lemon wedges, salad and heated bread rolls. Serves 4.

Sweet Chilli Prawns

These prawns taste so good that you won't mind the work involved in shelling them!

1.5 kg green prawns
2 tablespoons honey
2 tablespoons Thai Sweet chilli sauce
2 tablespoons lemon or lime juice
2 tablespoons oil
2 cloves garlic, finely chopped

Shell and devein the prawns, leaving the tails intact.

Combine the remaining ingredients and put into a plastic bag with the prepared prawns. Refrigerate for at least 1 hour, but preferably longer.

Barbecue prawns quickly, turning at least once, until prawns are cooked. Brush with any leftover marinade while they cook.

Serve immediately. Serves 6.

Skewered Satay Prawns

Take great care not to overcook these delicious morsels!

1.5 kg green prawns
1–2 tablespoons lemon or lime juice
1 tablespoon light soy sauce
1–2 tablespoons sesame oil
1 teaspoon ground cumin
2 cloves garlic, finely chopped
2 tablespoons chopped coriander leaves

Soak 12 bamboo skewers in cold water. Shell and devein the prawns, leaving the tails intact.

Combine remaining ingredients and marinate prawns for at least 1 hour, but preferably longer. Thread the marinated prawns onto the skewers.

Barbecue satays quickly, close to the heat, until prawns are cooked through. Brush with any leftover marinade during cooking.

Serve immediately with bought or homemade Satay Sauce (see page 11). Serves 6.

Vegetables, Salads and Accompaniments

If you barbecue often during warm weather, it is important that you balance your barbecue meals; include appetising vegetable dishes and salads as well as foods made from grains such as rice, pasta and bread. As well as being good for you, these will make all the difference to the colour, texture and flavour balance of your meal. Some of the recipes in this section are cooked on the barbecue, and others are cooked in the kitchen earlier in the day. If your children are not as interested in the foods which are served with meat as the meat itself, try serving the accompaniments before the meat is ready – while everybody is feeling very hungry!

Even if you have not barbecued vegetables very much in the past, I hope that you will experiment with some of the following suggestions. Remember that vegetables are naturally low in fat and need to be brushed with oil or butter mixtures before and during cooking. Long-cooking vegetables may be parcooked by microwaving or briefly boiling them before you take them outside to barbecue.

Watch heat levels, and the cooking times your vegetables need. In general the heat should not be so fierce, nor the cooking so long, that the vegetables burn, although a little charring is acceptable. Be prepared to turn the vegetables often to prevent burning.

Barbecue Potato Packs

It always takes a while to get a barbecue fire to the right stage for cooking meat over hot embers. Before this stage is reached you can start cooking Barbecue Packs because of their double aluminium foil coating. The packs are delicious and take 30–45 minutes to cook, depending on the heat of the fire.

For each serve tear off a piece of aluminium foil about 30 cm long. Fold in half so it is 15 cm wide. Smear a teaspoon of butter over central part of foil. Scrub then slice 1 or 2 new potatoes. Overlap the slices on the top half of the foil, leaving the edges clear. Sprinkle with salt, or onion or celery salt, then add a pinch of basil and marjoram (or other herbs). Put a few small pieces of butter on top then fold the foil over the potatoes, squeeze to push out most of the air, then turn the edges several times to seal the packages.

Place on a rack over the barbecue fire. Turn every few minutes for the first 15 minutes, then turn occasionally. Open a pack after 30 minutes to see whether potatoes are cooked. If not, reseal carefully.

Serve hot, warm or cool (but not chilled).

Barbecue Potato Packs

Barbecued Potatoes

When you barbecue precooked potatoes, all you have to do is brown and crisp the outside and heat them through.

Scrub large potatoes, simmer until just tender or microwave them as follows: scrub and quarter lengthways 8 fairly large potatoes, (about 1.5 kg). Put them in an oven bag with 25 g butter and 2 tablespoons water. Fasten bag with a rubber band, leaving a finger-sized opening. Microwave on High (100% power) for 12–20 minutes, repositioning potatoes in the bag twice, until potatoes are barely tender. Leave potatoes in the bag until you want to barbecue them. Put the potato quarters on a preheated oiled grill rack or a solid plate and turn to brown all sides evenly, brushing with flavoured butter or oil only if they burn. Barbecue time is likely to be 6–15 minutes, depending on conditions.

Barbecued New Potatoes

Microwave 750 g small potatoes with 1 tablespoon butter, 2 mint sprigs and 2 tablespoons water in an oven bag (refer instructions for Barbecued Potatoes, see above) for about 8 minutes. Thread them alone or with other vegetables on skewers. Brush with melted butter or Garlic Herb Butter (see page 76) before cooking on an oiled grill rack until nicely browned.

Barbecued Mushrooms

Mushrooms barbecue well without precooking. Toss in, or brush with Garlic Herb Butter (see page 76) or Mayonnaise (see page 66), or any oil-based dressing you like. Thread on presoaked bamboo skewers and cook over a grill rack or cook directly on the preheated hot plate. For interesting vegetable kebabs thread mushrooms with quick-cooking vegetables like cherry tomatoes, or with precooked vegetables like new potatoes, cubed cooked kumara, lightly precooked red, yellow and green capsicums, etc. Brush with Garlic Herb Butter or plain butter before barbecuing.

Barbecued Tomatoes

Small cherry tomatoes and quartered firm tomatoes may be skewered and barbecued with other quick-cooking vegetables. Large 'meaty' halved tomatoes cook quickly on a heated plate or on a grill rack. Watch tomatoes carefully, since they become very soft if barbecued too long.

Barbecued Eggplant

Thick slices or cubes of eggplant threaded on a skewer may be brushed with any well-flavoured oil and vinegar dressing, and barbecued until tender and browned. They may take longer than expected, and need frequent basting, so it is best to cook them alone, rather than on kebabs with quicker-cooking vegetables. Well-cooked eggplant has an interesting, meaty texture.

Cooked Vegetable Kebabs

Vegetables cut into 2 cm chunks that are precooked by brief boiling or microwaving, can be threaded on soaked bamboo or metal kebab skewers, brushed with butter, oil, or any flavoured butter, and browned lightly over a barbecue grill rack. Make colourful combinations of carrot, cauliflower, green, red or yellow capsicums, parsnip, pumpkin, kumara, zucchini and other summer squash, small whole onions or larger quartered onions. Brush your favourite glaze over kebabs, just before serving, if you like.

Left: Cooked Vegetable Kebabs
Right: Barbecued Corn Cobs

Barbecued Corn Cobs

Young corn cobs (grains have milky liquid inside when pierced with a fingernail) may be barbecued in their green husks. Soak whole corn cobs in a bucket of water for 10 minutes if you have the time – after soaking pull back husk and remove the silk, brush cobs with garlic or plain butter, then rewrap in husk. Cover with 10 cm wide band of aluminium foil if liked. Barbecue, turning frequently, until all sides are very hot and exposed husks char, about 5–10 minutes.

Don't barbecue very mature corn. Middle-aged cobs may be de-husked, brushed with butter and sealed in foil packages, and turned frequently on grill rack until grains are cooked. If preferred, precook cobs, butter, foil-wrap and reheat only on barbecue.

Serve as a vegetable or the main part of a barbecued meal with garlic mayonnaise, Herb Mayonnaise or Chilli Mayonnaise (see page 66).

Apple, Onion and Tomato Savoury

1 tablespoon butter
1 large or 2 medium-sized red onions
2–3 apples, cut in wedges
2–3 sage leaves, chopped
4 tomatoes, cut in wedges
½ teaspoon salt
1 tablespoon brown sugar
pepper
1 teaspoon cornflour

Melt the butter in a large pan, then cut the onions into halves, quarters, then eighths, lengthwise rather than crosswise. Cook onion in the butter, adding a tablespoonful of water, and covering the pan to encourage them to wilt and start cooking quickly.

Cut the apples into quarters then eighths, leaving them unpeeled if you like to see the colour of their skins, and do not mind the firmer texture. Stir into the partly cooked onion, and cover the pan again. Add the sage, tomatoes, salt, sugar and pepper to the pan when the apple wedges are tender, in 5–8 minutes, stirring them in carefully, so you do not break up the onion or apple.

Mix the cornflour with a little water, and stir it into the mixture to glaze it, as soon as the tomatoes have heated through. Do not let the tomatoes overcook and become soft.

Serve straightaway if possible, with barbecued sausages or pork fillet.

Roasted Capsicum Salad

Capsicums prepared like this have a wonderful flavour and an interesting texture. They are quite unlike raw capsicums.

> 4–6 plump, fleshy red, green, yellow or
> orange capsicums
> ¼ cup lemon juice
> ¼ cup olive oil
> freshly ground black pepper
> salt to taste

Use fresh, firm and fleshy capsicums. Heat whole capsicums under a grill, over a barbecue rack, or on a gas burner, keeping them close to the heat, and turning them as their skin blisters and blackens. Or roast in an oven heated to 220 °C for about 30 minutes.

When they have blackened in patches and have blistered fairly evenly, put them in a paper or plastic bag to stand for 5–10 minutes, then hold them, one at a time, under a cold tap and peel or cut off the skin. The flesh underneath should be brightly coloured and partly cooked. Quarter the peeled capsicums, and trim away the seeds and pith. Cut into even shapes, put them in a shallow dish, and coat with the lemon juice and oil, using less or more, depending on the amount of flesh you have. Refrigerate until you need them, up to two days.

Sprinkle with freshly ground pepper, add salt to taste, and serve at room temperature.

Pasta Salad

Pasta salads are popular but, unfortunately, they often do not taste as good as they look. A strongly flavoured dressing overcomes this.

> 250 g tortellini, spirals, or other pasta shapes
> 1 tablespoon oil
> ½ cup tomato purée
> 2 tablespoons sour cream
> ¼–½ cup olive oil
> 1 tablespoon wine vinegar
> 1 teaspoon sugar
> ½ teaspoon salt
> 1 teaspoon cumin
> ½ teaspoon oreganum, crumbled
> 1 or 2 firm tomatoes, diced (optional)
> 2 spring onions, thinly sliced white and
> green parts (optional)
> 2 tablespoons finely chopped parsley (optional)
> 1 stalk celery, sliced thinly (optional)
> ¼–½ cup small cubes of unpeeled telegraph
> cucumber (optional)
> ½ cup drained whole kernel corn (optional)

Cook the pasta until just tender in plenty of boiling, lightly salted water with the tablespoon of oil, then drain thoroughly. Take care not to undercook or overcook the pasta if you want a good salad.

Mix together the next eight ingredients, using olive oil for its flavour if possible. Stir the dressing gently into the hot, drained pasta, and allow to stand for at least 15 minutes. During this time the pasta will absorb a lot of the dressing. Refrigerate the salad until you want to serve it.

Just before serving add the tomatoes, spring onions, and any other optional ingredients, and stir into the salad. Serves 4–6.

Quick Salad Ideas

• Florence fennel (finocchio) quartered lengthways, simmered until tender, then left to stand in French or Italian dressing.

• Globe artichokes boiled in water to cover until the petals pull off easily, then served with mayonnaise for the petals to be dipped into, and the soft part of the petal scraped off with the teeth.

• Whole young beans boiled until barely tender, then turned in enough garlic-flavoured dressing to coat them.

• Cooked carrots, whole, sliced lengthwise or in rounds, turned in a mixture of lemon juice, oil, salt, sugar and mustard, with lots of chopped parsley.

• Asparagus, cooked until just tender, with plain or orange-flavoured mayonnaise for dipping.

• Zucchini, chopped and boiled until tender-crisp, coated with (olive) oil, freshly ground pepper, and a little lemon juice if you like.

• Beans, cauliflower, zucchini, celery, carrots, etc cooked 'a la Grecque', served at room temperature in their cooking liquid.

Top: Roasted Capsicum Salad
Below: Pasta Salad

'Roasted' Vegetable Salad

'Roasted' Vegetable Salad

Choose a colourful mixture of seasonal vegetables such as red onions, eggplants, zucchini, red and yellow capsicums, etc. Cut them into chunky pieces. Quarter onions so pieces are held together by the root.

Brush with Seasoned Oil and barbecue about 12 cm from the heat, turning frequently so vegetables cook before they burn. Allow vegetables to brown but not burn on their edges.

Seasoned Oil:
½ cup olive oil
2 cloves garlic, peeled
6 basil leaves, chopped
2 tablespoons fresh thyme
2 tablespoons fresh rosemary

Put all ingredients in a food processor fitted with its metal chopping blade. Process until finely chopped. Allow to stand for at least 10 minutes then strain, discarding flavourings.

Potato Salad with Lemon Mayonnaise

With home-made mayonnaise used as the dressing, this potato salad is wonderful. Alter flavourings to suit yourself.

1 kg small new potatoes, approximately
3 eggs, hard-boiled
½ cup Mayonnaise (see page 66)
2 tablespoons lemon juice
1–2 tablespoons chopped tarragon, basil, spring onions or parsley (optional)

Quarter or halve the potatoes lengthways, and boil until just cooked, adding water as required. Hard-boil the eggs with the potatoes if desired. Drain the potatoes and leave to cool.

If you are making the mayonnaise, use lemon juice rather than vinegar. To make the dressing for this salad, measure out ½ cup of mayonnaise and add the extra lemon juice and chopped herbs. Peel the eggs, then chop two of them. In a large bowl toss together the cooled potatoes, the mayonnaise and the chopped egg.

Pile into a serving bowl and garnish by finely grating the remaining egg over the top. Refrigerate until required.

Serve with a leafy green salad as part of a summer meal. Serves 4–6.

Spicy Bean and Rice Salad

This rice, bean and vegetable mixture is especially good served with Cuban Chicken (see page 13).

2 tablespoons olive oil
1 large onion, chopped
2 cloves garlic, finely chopped
1 each red, yellow and green capsicum, deseeded and chopped
leftover marinade from Cuban Chicken
1 cup cooked rice
1 cup cooked kidney beans (310 g can)
½ teaspoon salt
425 g can tomatoes, roughly chopped
2 tablespoons olive oil
¼ cup chopped fresh coriander leaves or parsley

Heat the first measure of oil in a large frypan. Add the onion, garlic, and capsicum. Cover lightly and cook over a medium heat for 4–6 minutes until onion is translucent and capsicum is tender. Add all remaining ingredients except for the coriander or parsley. Heat to evaporate liquid, cooking for about 5 minutes.

Just before serving, stir the coriander or parsley through the mixture. Serves 4–6.

Spinach Salad

400–500 g spinach
4–6 rashers bacon
olive oil
¼ teaspoon salt, approximately
1 teaspoon sugar
2–3 teaspoons Dijon-type mustard
2 tablespoons wine vinegar
200 g button mushrooms
a few canned water chestnuts (optional)
avocado (optional)
½–1 cup small croutons (see page 67)

Wash the spinach carefully in a sink of cold water. Drain, then break the large leaves off the stems, leaving the central rib attached to the stem (so each leaf is in two halves, lengthwise). Leave small leaves whole. Handle the leaves carefully to avoid bruising them. Roll in a teatowel and refrigerate, making sure that the leaves are dry before using them in the salad.

Grill the bacon until crisp, reserving the fat that drains off it. Remove rinds and chop bacon into bits and set aside.

To make the dressing, measure the bacon fat and make it up to about 6 tablespoons with olive oil. Mix it in a pan with the salt, sugar, mustard and vinegar and leave to stand at room temperature until the salad is required.

Wash and dry the mushrooms, and slice them. Drain canned water chestnuts if using and slice them. (Keep remaining water chestnuts in a jar of cold water in the refrigerator. If you change the water regularly, they will last for weeks.)

Just before serving, warm the dressing to bloodheat. Put the cold dry spinach, bacon and mushrooms in a large serving bowl or plastic bag, then pour the dressing over them, and toss gently until the spinach is coated. Arrange in individual bowls and sprinkle generously with croutons. Serve promptly. Serves 4–6.

Note: If including avocado, slice and coat with lemon juice, and add to the already tossed salad.

Cumin Bean Salad

This is a salad which may be kept in a covered container in the refrigerator for a week and served as the main part of a dinner or light meal, whenever you want something quick and easy.

    4 cups cooked drained dried beans, or if
        preferred use canned drained beans
    1 cup chopped cooked green beans
    ½–1 cup diced green capsicum
    1 cup diced celery
    1 cup diced tomato, approximately

Cumin Dressing:
    ½ cup corn or soya oil
    ¼ cup wine or cider vinegar
    2 teaspoons ground cumin
    1–2 teaspoons onion powder
    ¼ teaspoon salt
    2 teaspoons dried oreganum
    ½–1 teaspoon garlic powder
    black pepper
    hot pepper sauce to taste

To prepare the salad using dried beans:
Choose and measure the beans, keeping each type separate. You want a total of 1 ¼ cups which when cooked will yield approximately 4 cups. Place each variety of bean in an unpunctured oven bag. Pour into each bag enough boiling water to cover the beans and leave to stand for 1 hour. Drain, pour over about a cup of boiling water for every ¼ cup of beans, and cook, standing the oven bags in one big bowl or other container, in the microwave oven. Alternatively, cook in separate saucepans on the stove top. The cooking time of the beans in both cases will be 1–1 ½ hours. In the microwave use Medium (50%) power. It is important that the beans are cooked until really tender. To test for this, the beans should be easily squashed between the thumb and index finger, or against the roof of the mouth with the tongue.

Put the drained beans, capsicum and celery in a large covered container.

Place all the dressing ingredients in a screw-top jar. Shake well. Add the dressing and mix to coat. Cover and refrigerate for at least 2 hours before serving.

When required, bring to room temperature, add tomato to the amount you want to serve, and toss to mix. Serves 6.

Greek Summer Salad

This salad makes a good first course before any lamb or chicken barbecue.

    1 small to medium-sized cucumber
    4 large or more small tomatoes
    1 small red onion
    dried oreganum
    50 g feta cheese, approximately
    10 black olives, approximately
    olive oil
    black pepper
    lemon wedges (optional)

Greek Summer Salad (left) and Cumin Bean Salad

Peel the green outer skin from the cucumber, using a potato peeler. Cut it in half lengthwise and scoop out the seedy area, using a teaspoon. Cut into 1 cm chunks and place in a salad bowl. Top with thickly sliced, cubed or whole small tomatoes, then with rings of onion. (If mild red onions are not available, use spring onions, or soak slices of ordinary yellow onion in water for an hour before draining and drying them.)

Sprinkle the surface of the salad with dried oreganum, then add small cubes or thin slices of feta cheese, and toss the black olives over the top. Dribble olive oil over the salad, and add black pepper to taste.

Squeeze the lemon wedge over the salad if you like, or eat it without the lemon juice. Beware of adding salt until you have eaten some of the rather salty feta cheese and the black olives in between mouthfuls of the other vegetables. Serves 2.

Note: As the seasons change, use other vegetables, as the Greeks do. Replace the cucumber with chopped lettuce or light-coloured cabbage heart, and add green and red capsicums if they are of good quality, and plentiful.

Bean Sprout and Carrot Salad (left), and Bean Salad

Bean Salad

This is a useful make-ahead salad. It will keep well in the refrigerator for several days. Mixed dried beans make a colourful nutritious salad. They need to be soaked before cooking to prevent the quicker cooking beans 'mushing' before the others are ready.

1 ½ cups mixed dried salad beans
½ cup wine vinegar
½ cup sugar
½ cup oil
½ cup liquid from beans (see below)
1 teaspoon salt
1 cup chopped red, yellow or green
   capsicums (or a combination of all three)
½ cup chopped celery
1 medium-sized red onion, chopped

Soak the salad beans in 1 litre of warm or cold water for 8 hours, then discard water and replace it with 1 litre of fresh water (do not add salt). Bring to the boil, cover, and simmer very gently for 1–2 hours or until the longest-cooking beans are tender. Drain, putting aside about a cup of the liquid, since some is needed for the dressing.

To make the dressing, combine the vinegar, sugar, oil, ½ cup of the cooking liquid and salt. Pour this mixture over the warm or hot drained beans.

Chop the remaining vegetables so they are in pieces about the same size as the beans. Add to the salad when it is cold or nearly cold. The vegetables and beans should be covered with dressing. Make up extra dressing using the same proportions as before, if necessary, or add more of only some of the dressing ingredients if you want a modified flavour. Refrigerate for at least several hours before serving.

To serve, drain the dressing from the beans and vegetables. Serves 6–8.

Bean Sprout and Carrot Salad

3 slices bread, preferably wholemeal
1 tablespoon olive oil
2 large carrots, coarsely grated
1 cup bean sprouts
½ cup salted peanuts
½ cup raisins or sultanas
¼ cup finely chopped parsley
2 tablespoons olive or other oil
2 teaspoons sesame oil
2 tablespoons lemon juice
½ teaspoon salt
1 teaspoon sugar

Cut the bread into 5 mm cubes. Heat the oil in a small frypan, toss the cubes in it, then cook until they are crisp and golden brown. Cool.

Put the prepared carrots, bean sprouts, peanuts, raisins and parsley in a salad bowl. Cover and refrigerate if you are doing the preparation ahead of time.

Mix together the second measure of oil, the sesame oil, lemon juice, salt and sugar and set aside until needed.

Just before serving toss half the croutons through the other ingredients, add the dressing and toss again, then sprinkle with the remaining croutons. Serve immediately. Serves 6–8.

Pilaf

Particularly nice served with lamb kebabs.

2 tablespoons oil or butter
1 medium-sized onion, chopped
1 cup ribbon noodles, broken into
  1–2 cm pieces
½ cup burghul (bulghar)
2 cups chicken stock
1 cinnamon stick

Heat the oil or butter in a large frypan and cook the onion until golden brown.

Add the broken noodles and burghul, and cook until lightly browned. Add the chicken stock (use 2 cups water and 2 teaspoons instant stock if necessary) and the cinnamon stick and cook over a medium heat for about 10 minutes, or until the liquid is absorbed and the noodles and burghul are tender. Add a little extra water if the liquid disappears too soon.

Toss with a fork and serve immediately for best flavour. Serves 4–6.

Tabbouleh

1 cup burghul (bulghar)
425 g can Chunky Tomatoes and Onions
½ cup water
2–3 tablespoons olive or other oil
1 tablespoon lemon juice
2 spring onions
2–3 tablespoons chopped fresh mint
¼–½ cup chopped parsley
¼ teaspoon salt, approximately

Bring burghul, the canned tomatoes and onions, and the water to the boil, then remove from the heat and stir in the oil and lemon juice. While the tomato mixture cools, chop the spring onions, using both the white and green parts, the mint and the parsley.

Mix these flavourings gently through the cool mixture. Add salt and any other seasonings to taste. Refrigerate in a covered container until required.

Just before serving, mix lightly, adding a little extra oil and/or water if dry, and adjust the seasonings. Serves 4–6.

Variations: Add any optional ingredients, eg chopped red, green or yellow capsicums, black olives, celery, cucumber or a little pesto.

Salad Dressings

Be adventurous with the salad dressings that follow. Use them to add zing and zest to a variety of plainly cooked hot or cold vegetables. Try dressings with all sorts of salad vegetables and with ripe fruits in season.

Italian Dressing

2 teaspoons cornflour
½ cup water
2–3 teaspoons onion pulp
1 small clove garlic, finely chopped
1 teaspoon dried oreganum, crumbled
1 teaspoon mixed mustard
½ teaspoon paprika
1 teaspoon salt
1 tablespoon sugar
1 tablespoon tomato paste
¼ cup wine vinegar
½ cup olive or other oil

Mix together the cornflour and water in a small pot and bring to the boil, stirring until thick. Cool slightly and put into a screw-top jar with the remaining ingredients. Shake until well combined.

Refrigerate for up to a month. Shake well before use.

Mayonnaise

This is an extremely useful and delicious sauce which is easy and quick to make in a food processor or blender.

    1 egg
    ½ teaspoon salt
    ½ teaspoon sugar
    1 teaspoon Dijon mustard
    2 tablespoons wine vinegar
    1 cup corn or olive oil, approximately

Measure the first five ingredients into a blender or food processor. Turn on and pour in the oil in a thin stream until the mayonnaise is as thick as you like.

Store in a covered container in the refrigerator for up to 2–3 weeks.

Variations:

Garlic Mayonnaise: Add one or two cloves of garlic before adding the oil. Leave to stand for an hour to soften the flavour before using.

Herb Mayonnaise: Add about ¼ cup roughly chopped parsley, and 1–2 teaspoons of one or more fresh or dried herbs such as basil, oreganum, thyme, dill, etc, before adding the oil.

Chilli Mayonnaise: Add ½–1 teaspoon chilli powder, 1 teaspoon dried oreganum, 1–2 teaspoons ground cumin, and 1 chopped clove of garlic before adding the oil. The flavour improves and becomes hotter after it stands for several hours.

Herbed Vinaigrette

    ¾ cup olive oil
    ¼ cup wine vinegar
    1 teaspoon mixed mustard
    3–4 tablespoons chopped fresh herbs
    1 clove garlic, finely chopped
    ½ teaspoon salt
    ½ teaspoon sugar
    pepper to taste

Put all ingredients into a food processor or blender and process until well combined, or shake well in a screw-top jar. Refrigerate in a covered container for up to 2 weeks. Shake well before using.

Use on raw vegetables, or hot or cold cooked vegetables.

Sesame Dressing

    2 cloves garlic, finely chopped
    1 teaspoon grated fresh root ginger
    1 tablespoon dark soy sauce
    1 tablespoon light soy sauce
    1 teaspoon sesame oil
    2 teaspoons sugar
    2 teaspoons rice vinegar
    2 tablespoons finely chopped fresh
      coriander leaves

Combine all ingredients in a screw-top jar and shake well to combine.

Tomato Dressing

    2 spring onions, chopped
    ½ cup tomato purée
    3 tablespoons wine vinegar
    2 teaspoons mixed mustard
    2 teaspoons sugar
    ½ teaspoon salt
    1 cup olive or other oil

Combine all ingredients in a screw-top jar and shake until well combined. Refrigerate for up to 1 week. Shake well before using.

Lemon Honey Dressing

    ¼ cup lemon juice
    2 tablespoons light soy sauce
    2 tablespoons salad oil
    2 tablespoons honey
    1 tablespoon Dijon mustard
    1 tablespoon sesame oil
    1 teaspoon finely grated lemon rind
    1 clove garlic, finely chopped

Combine all ingredients and either process until smooth using a food processor or shake well in a screw-top jar.

Very good over diced fresh fruit, such as apples, pears, peaches, nectarines, etc. Or use over finely shredded raw vegetables, or lightly cooked stir-fried asparagus, green beans or other vegetables.

Croutons

50 g butter
4–5 teaspoons of a mixture of flavoured salts and/or instant stocks, approximately
8 cups of 5 mm cubes of stale bread, bread rolls or French bread

Melt the butter in a roasting pan or grilling pan. Mix with it the flavourings you intend to use. Choose from onion, garlic, and celery salt, and/or instant chicken, green herbs and bacon stock. Use level measuring teaspoons (do not be tempted to use more than 5 teaspoons or the croutons will be too salty).

Tip the bread cubes into the hot butter and mix well, straightaway, so you get the butter evenly through the mixture.

Put the pan of buttered cubes at least 10 cm away from the grill and lightly brown the cubes until they are a light, even colour and quite crisp. Do not hurry this step, since the bread must dry out completely. Turn off the grill and leave the cubes to cool down, almost to room temperature.

For long storage, heat several clean screw-top jars in a low oven until they are too hot to hold without an oven cloth. Wash and dry plastic lids, and stand metal lids in boiling water until you need them. Spoon the cool croutons into the hot jars and screw on the dry lids immediately.

Makes enough croutons to fill a 2-litre ice cream container.

Barbecue Bread

This bread is always wildly popular with teenagers!

4 cloves garlic
100 g soft butter
2 cups grated cheese
3 tablespoons tomato sauce
1 tablespoon tomato paste (optional)

Mix all ingredients in the food processor using the metal chopping blade, adding the tomato paste if you like a pronounced tomato colour and flavour.

Cut a loaf of any shape into slices, without cutting through the bottom crust. Spread as much filling as you like between the slices, wrap in aluminium foil and bake at 180 °C for 10–30 minutes depending on the dimensions of the loaf. Open foil so top can brown when loaf has heated through fairly evenly, or cook over the barbecue rack, turning often until heated through.

Barbecue Treats for Vegetarians

Don't forget about vegetarians when you plan a barbecue for a group of young people. Vegetarians as well as meat-eaters will enjoy interesting vegetable dishes, but it is a nice idea to include on your menu some kebabs made with tofu and/or polenta, and some no-meat burgers. Remember that many meat-eaters are also fond of polenta – so be sure to make plenty!

Marinated Tofu Kebabs

When left to stand in a well-flavoured marinade, tofu absorbs its flavour.

Square slabs of marinated tofu, sautéed in a teaspoon or so of oil, make good burgers or toasted sandwiches. Cubes, sautéed for a few minutes on all sides, may be threaded on sticks with vegetables to make kebabs, which are then carefully grilled or barbecued. Although the outside will be quite firm and crusty, the inside will keep its original soft texture. Use tofu which is firm, or extra-firm, or the tofu may fall apart when skewered.

500 g extra-firm tofu
¼ cup corn or soya oil
¼ cup lemon juice
¼ cup dark soy sauce
2 large cloves garlic, chopped
1 tablespoon sesame oil
1 teaspoon dried oreganum
hot pepper sauce to taste
selection of vegetables, eg mushrooms,
  cherry tomatoes, red and green capsicums,
  zucchini or aubergine
mayonnaise (optional)

Drain the tofu, cut into 2 cm cubes, and leave to stand while you prepare the marinade.

Measure the remaining ingredients into an unpunctured plastic bag, using enough hot pepper sauce to give the hotness you like. Stand the bag in a shallow baking pan and place the tofu in it so that the cubes lie flat. Suck out the air, so that the tofu is surrounded by the marinade, and fasten with a rubber band. Leave for at least 4 hours and up to 48 hours (for maximum flavour), turning the bag occasionally. Reserve marinade.

Brown the drained tofu cubes in a non-stick pan with a few drops of oil over a moderate to high heat for 30–40 seconds per side.

Cut the capsicum into squares and the zucchini and/or aubergine into cubes, and turn in the marinade with the mushrooms and tomatoes.

Thread the lightly sautéed tofu cubes on skewers with the vegetables.

Cook over the barbecue rack or in a flat grill basket for 5–10 minutes per side turning once, and brushing with mayonnaise or with extra marinade if desired.

Serve the kebabs on rice, noodles, burghul, or in split, lightly toasted bread rolls with tomato sauce or chilli sauce. Serves 4–6.

Marinated Tofu Kebabs

Grilled Polenta Kebabs

Polenta is a type of corn porridge made from corn meal. The thick, well-flavoured porridge is left to set, then cut into cubes and browned lightly in a non-stick pan.

The browned cubes, threaded on skewers with vegetables, may be barbecued outdoors or heated on a small electric table-top grill/barbecue.

2 cups water
1 teaspoon salt, approximately
1 teaspoon fresh thyme, basil and oreganum or ½ teaspoon of each dried
1 cup coarse yellow corn meal
1 cup grated cheddar cheese or ¼–½ cup grated parmesan cheese

Bring the water and salt to the boil. Add the dried or fresh herbs. Sprinkle the corn meal into the water while stirring thoroughly. Keep stirring, over a low to moderate heat, for about 5 minutes, until very thick. Remove from the heat and stir in the grated cheese. (The polenta may seem salty at first, but this saltiness diminishes on standing.)

Pour into a buttered or oiled 20 cm square pan, and leave to cool for about 30 minutes. Turn out and cut into 2 cm cubes.

Brown polenta cubes on all sides in a non-stick pan with a little butter or oil. Thread on skewers, alternated with vegetables, and barbecue when required. Serves 4.

Variation: Pour polenta into a round pan, then cut in wedges. Brown on the solid plate of a barbecue, and serve with fried eggs, mushrooms, tomatoes, etc. Make without cheese for those on vegan diets.

Barbecued Nut Cutlets

As long as you handle these carefully, they can be barbecued quite successfully.

½ cup unblanched peanuts
½ cup cashew nuts or almonds
½ cup pine nuts
½ cup sunflower seeds
2 slices bread
1 medium-sized onion
1 carrot
2 eggs
2 teaspoons dark soy sauce
½ teaspoon garlic salt
½ teaspoon ground cumin
½ teaspoon chilli powder (optional)
1 tablespoon chopped coriander leaves (optional)
black pepper
1–2 tablespoons oil

Place the nuts and sunflower seeds in a food processor and chop until the mixture resembles coarse breadcrumbs. Transfer the chopped nuts to a separate bowl. Process the bread into crumbs and add to the chopped nuts.

Peel and quarter the onion, roughly chop the carrot and process until finely chopped. Add the eggs, soy sauce and seasonings and process briefly. Combine with the chopped nuts and breadcrumbs. Mix thoroughly, then divide the mixture into eight portions and shape into patties.

Brush patties with the oil and cook in a hinged flat wire basket for about 5 minutes per side. Alternatively, cook patties on an oiled solid barbecue plate for a similar time.

Serve with sweet chilli sauce or satay sauce. Makes 8 patties.

Mushroom Burgers

These burgers are very popular with mushroom lovers. The recipe is especially good made with older mushrooms that have dark gills as they have a stronger flavour.

2 medium-sized onions, chopped
2 cloves garlic, chopped
2 tablespoons oil
350 g flat brown-gilled mushrooms, finely chopped
2 cups fresh wholemeal breadcrumbs
2 teaspoons cornflour
¼ cup fresh chopped parsley
2 teaspoons nutritional yeast (optional)
2 eggs
1 tablespoon lemon juice (juice of ½ a lemon)
1 teaspoon dark soy sauce
1 teaspoon chopped fresh thyme (optional)

Sauté the onion and garlic in the oil until the onion softens. Add the mushrooms and continue cooking until they turn soft and dark.

Tip the onion and mushroom mixture into a medium-sized bowl, and add the remaining ingredients. Mix well, using your hands if necessary. Add some more breadcrumbs if the mixture seems too wet. Divide into four equal portions and then shape each quarter into a 10 cm pattie.

Cook patties in a little oil or butter, on a solid barbecue plate, until lightly browned on each side and firm when pressed in the middle. Makes 8 patties.

Note: If preferred, precook the patties in a pan, inside, before they are needed then reheat in a flat wire grilling basket over the barbecue.

Beanburgers

If you make this recipe with canned beans, use scant measures of the seasonings as the beans already have some added salt.

2 cups cooked kidney beans, approximately
1 large onion, finely chopped
1 tablespoon butter or oil
1 teaspoon oreganum
1 teaspoon ground cumin
1 teaspoon curry powder
1 teaspoon salt
1 teaspoon sugar
1 egg
¼ cup dried breadcrumbs, approximately

Drain the cooked beans thoroughly.

In a frypan cook over a medium heat the onion in the butter or oil for about 15 minutes until evenly browned and tender. Stir in all the seasonings and remove from the heat. Mash the drained beans with a fork and add to the seasoned onion. Mix in the egg with a fork, then add enough dried breadcrumbs to make a mixture just firm enough to form into eight soft patties. Coat the patties with remaining crumbs.

Cook patties in a film of oil on a solid barbecue plate for about 10 minutes per side. Serve with tomato relish, sauce, etc., in hamburger buns or with salads or cooked vegetables. Serves 4.

Note: To cook beans, pour 1 litre hot water over 1 cup dried kidney beans and leave them to stand for at least 1 hour, or up to 24 hours. Drain, add 1 litre fresh water, boil briskly for 15 minutes, then simmer for about an hour or until tender enough to crush with your tongue on the roof of your mouth. Do not add salt while cooking beans, but add garlic and herbs for extra flavour if you like.

71

Brown Lentil Burgers

These burgers take a little longer to make than some other vegetarian burgers, but they have a good firm texture, much like that of conventional burgers.

½ cup brown lentils
1 bay leaf
1 teaspoon finely chopped garlic
2 medium-sized onions, finely chopped
2 cloves garlic, finely chopped
2 tablespoons oil or butter
1 tablespoon parsley
½ teaspoon basil
½ teaspoon marjoram
¼ teaspoon (a large pinch) thyme
1 teaspoon salt
black pepper to taste
½ cup fresh wholemeal breadcrumbs
2 eggs
2 tablespoons tomato paste
2 teaspoons dark soy sauce
½ cup flour

Simmer the lentils with the bay leaf in 3 cups of unsalted water and 1 teaspoon chopped garlic in a covered pot until they are tender. Remove them from the heat, drain, and discard the bay leaf.

Sauté the onion and garlic in the oil or butter until the onion is soft and clear. Add the herbs, salt and pepper.

Tip the cooked, drained lentils into a large bowl, add the seasoned onion and garlic, then mix in the remaining ingredients.

Divide the mixture into eight even-sized portions. Shape each portion into a 10–12 cm pattie, wetting your hands with cold water to prevent the mixture sticking. If the mixture won't hold its shape, add a few more breadcrumbs or a little more flour until it does.

Cook patties in a thin film of oil on a solid barbecue plate until browned on each side and firm when pressed in the middle. Serves 4.

Dry-Mix Vegeburgers

It seems unbelievable that you can moisten a dry bean mix, leave it to stand for 15 minutes then cook it as a burger! What's more, the resulting burgers have a better flavour than those made from any commercial mix I have tried (and you can keep the mix in an airtight jar for up to 3 months, although it loses a little of its flavour on long storage). However, do not try to grind dried peas and beans in a flimsy plastic blender or coffee grinder (I found the sturdy coffee-grinder attachment on my food processor to be the most effective method – it makes a terrible noise, but the convenience of the completed product makes it all worthwhile!).

Burger Mix:
½ cup chick peas
½ cup soybeans
½ cup peanuts (raw) or sunflower kernels
¼ cup toasted sesame seeds
½ cup rolled oats
¼ cup pea flour
1 tablespoon parsley
1 teaspoon salt
¼ cup wheat germ (optional)
1 tablespoon nutritional yeast (optional)

Burgers:
1 cup Burger Mix
½ cup water
½ cup finely grated carrot
1 clove garlic, finely chopped (optional)
2 teaspoons dark soy sauce
1–2 tablespoons oil

Measure the first four ingredients for the Burger Mix into a bowl and mix together. Using a sturdy blender or food processor grind half a cup of this mixture at a time until it is the consistency of dry breadcrumbs.

Combine the freshly ground bean mixture with the remaining ingredients. Store in an airtight jar until desired.

When ready to make burgers, mix everything except the cooking oil together and allow to stand for 15 minutes. Divide mixture into four portions and shape into patties.

Cook patties in a thin film of oil on a solid barbecue plate until browned on each side. Makes 4 patties.

Dry-Mix Vegeburgers

Marinades, Sauces, Salsas and Relishes

There are times when it is enjoyable to cook an elaborate barbecue recipe, but there are many other occasions when you might want to cook meat as plainly as possible with the minimum of fuss and bother. On the latter occasions it is good to have a selection of home-made glazes, sauces, salsas, relishes, pickles and chutneys to produce that will liven up plainly cooked foods. Some are meant to be eaten within a few days, but others will keep for months.

Some of these mixtures have been used with various meats, fish and vegetables throughout the book. They are grouped together here – not only for convenience, but also to make comparisons when you are choosing which one will best suit the occasion.

Sesame Onion Marinade

2 tablespoons light soy sauce
1 tablespoon onion juice (scraped from the cut surface of an onion cut through its equator)
1–2 teaspoons sesame oil

Stir together all ingredients. Leave chosen meat or fish (suitable for chicken, all meats and fish) to stand in marinade before barbecuing, and brush on during cooking if desired.

Soy and Sherry Dip

¼ cup light soy sauce
¼ cup sherry
2 tablespoons sugar
1 garlic clove, crushed

Simmer all ingredients together until reduced to half original volume. Brush over any quick-cooking meat during the cooking process and drizzle some over before serving.

Lemon and Garlic Dipping Sauce

2 tablespoons lemon juice
2 cloves garlic
1 small dried chilli
2 tablespoons sugar
2 tablespoons fish or light soy sauce
2 tablespoons hot water
1 spring onion, finely chopped

Process all ingredients except for spring onion together until finely chopped. Strain through a sieve and add spring onion. Use as a dipping sauce or, just before serving, pour a few drops over barbecued fish, shellfish, lamb and vegetables.

Apricot Mustard Glaze

2 tablespoons apricot jam
2 teaspoons mixed Dijon-type mustard
1 tablespoon dark or light soy sauce
a little sherry or orange juice for thinning

Warm together the jam, mustard and the soy sauce. Thin with sherry or orange juice if necessary, until it is a good consistency to brush over nearly cooked lamb, chicken or pork.

Minted Yoghurt Sauce

½ cup plain yoghurt
1 tablespoon lemon juice
½ teaspoon salt
½ teaspoon ground cumin
½ teaspoon sugar
1 garlic clove, mashed and chopped
2–3 tablespoons finely chopped mint

Stir together all ingredients and leave to stand for at least half an hour. Use some to marinate your chosen cut of lamb, and the rest as a sauce over the barbecued lamb.

Hollandaise Sauce

Once thickened, this sauce is remarkably good-natured and stable as long as you don't heat it above bath temperature.

2 egg yolks
1 tablespoon lemon juice
100 g butter
1 teaspoon of finely grated orange rind (optional)

Place the egg yolks and lemon juice in a food processor fitted with a metal chopping blade.

Cut the butter into cubes and melt it in the microwave oven in a covered microwavable jug on High (100% power) for 2–3 minutes or until it's very hot, popping and bubbling vigorously. Before it has time to cool, turn on the food processor and pour the very hot butter in a steady stream onto the egg yolks. The hot butter should cook and thicken the egg yolks. Transfer sauce to a small bowl and cover.

Reheat by standing the bowl of sauce in a larger container of bath-temperature water for about 15 minutes, stirring occasionally. (Do not be tempted to use hot water or the sauce will curdle.)

Note: In cold weather run very hot water over the bowl and blades of the processor before putting in the egg and lemon juice.

Garlic Herb Butter

3–4 peeled garlic cloves
1 cup parsley sprigs
½ teaspoon thyme, dill, sage or basil
200 g soft but not melted butter
a little lemon rind
1–2 tablespoons lemon juice
black pepper
hot pepper sauce to taste

Chop together very finely in a food processor the garlic, parsley and herbs. Add the butter, lemon rind and juice and season with pepper and pepper sauce. Process to mix, then refrigerate in a covered dish until needed (will keep up to two weeks). Melt small quantities to brush over fish, or skinned chicken breasts, or vegetable kebabs before barbecuing.

Salsa

'Salsa' is simply the Mexican word for sauce. To me, this sauce is usually uncooked, or very briefly cooked, and is based on tomato or raw fruit. Flavoured with different herbs, it is carefully seasoned, and usually has some chilli added. My salsas are best eaten a few hours after they are made, although they will keep for a few days in the refrigerator. If they are kept too long, however, they lose their 'oomph'.

Tomato Salsa

Unless fresh tomatoes are at their best, I used canned tomatoes in this salsa, since they often have a better flavour.

1 small onion (preferably red), cut into quarters
1 spring onion
1 (400 g) can whole peeled tomatoes in brine or juice, drained
¼–½ cup loosely packed fresh basil or fresh coriander leaves
½ teaspoon salt
1 teaspoon sugar
1–2 tablespoons wine vinegar
1 teaspoon hot pepper sauce
1 tablespoon tomato paste, approximately (optional)

Put quartered onions into a food processor with both the green top and the bottom of the spring onion. Using the metal chopping blade, process briefly to chop the onions (overprocessing will pulp the onions and the salsa will lose its texture).

Add the drained tomatoes and remaining ingredients and again process briefly, just until the tomatoes and herbs are chopped, but not puréed.

Taste, and add more vinegar if necessary, and more hot pepper sauce if you require a 'hotter' flavour. Add tomato paste if you want a stronger tomato flavour.

Allow the salsa to stand for about 1 hour before serving to allow the flavours to blend. The mixture will thicken on standing, and should be stirred well before serving. Makes about 1 ½ cups.

Fruit Salsa

This fruit salsa is a cross between a salad and a relish. The fresh fruit is coated with a sharp-flavoured, tangy mixture of lime (essential – don't substitute lemon juice!) and fresh ginger. The fresh coriander leaves add their distinctive flavour so the mixture is quite unlike a bland fruit salad!

1 cup fresh peaches, kiwifruit, mango or melon, or any fresh seasonal fruit with good flavour and texture
¼ cup lime juice
1 teaspoon grated fresh root ginger
1 tablespoon chopped coriander leaves
salt
hot pepper sauce (optional)

Slice the fresh fruit into a dish. Mix the lime juice, grated ginger and chopped coriander together and mix them gently through the fruit to coat all the pieces. Taste and add a little salt and hot pepper sauce if you like. Refrigerate for up to 1 hour then serve with freshly cooked fish cakes.

If fresh coriander is hard to get, use a little mint and/or very thinly sliced spring onion.

Kiwifruit Salsa

2 cups ripe kiwifruit, chopped or sliced
¼ cup onion or shallots, finely chopped or sliced
¼ cup chopped red capsicum
1 clove garlic, crushed
½ cup basil leaves, finely chopped
¼ teaspoon very finely chopped red or green chilli
1 teaspoon ground cumin
¼ cup lime or lemon juice
salt and freshly ground black pepper to taste

Combine all ingredients, stirring them together so the kiwifruit keeps its shape. Refrigerate for up to 24 hours in a covered container, or fold through cooked fish, using amounts to suit yourself.

Note: Take care when you use fresh chillies. Mixtures containing thinly sliced chilli get hotter on standing. If in doubt, use a pinch of chilli powder or a teaspoonful of hot pepper sauce instead.

Mango Salsa

2 cups diced mango (or any other seasonal fruit such as peaches, nectarines, paw-paw, etc)
2 tablespoons finely chopped fresh coriander leaves
1 tablespoon lime juice
½–1 teaspoon finely chopped fresh green chilli
½ teaspoon salt

Chop fruit into fine dice. Combine the remaining ingredients in a screw-top jar and shake well. Just before serving, gently toss the fruit in the dressing to coat.

Cashew and Coriander Salsa

This is an interesting salsa to serve with any plainly cooked fish.

½ cup chopped coriander leaves
1 bottled jalapeño pepper
¼ cup raw cashew nuts
1 teaspoon ground cumin
1 teaspoon brown sugar
½ teaspoon salt
½ cup skinned, cubed ripe tomato

Put all ingredients except tomatoes into a food processor bowl and process to a paste. Add the cubed tomatoes and chop briefly (salsa thins down when the tomato is added). Eat the day it is made, refrigerating until ready to serve.

Kiwi Relish

2 cloves garlic
2 spring onions, roughly chopped
1 teaspoon green peppercorns in brine, drained and crushed
2 tablespoons wine vinegar
1 tablespoon Thai yellow chilli sauce
1 teaspoon salt
¼ cup coriander leaves, chopped
4 kiwifruit, halved and quartered

Peel the garlic and put in the food processor with the spring onion and the green peppercorns. Process until finely chopped. Add the vinegar, chilli sauce and salt and process to mix, then add the coriander leaves and the quartered kiwifruit. Process carefully, using the pulse button, until the kiwifruit and coriander leaves are fairly finely and evenly chopped.

Leave to stand for 1–2 hours before use for best flavour. Refrigerate for up to 2 days, if desired.

Maharajah's Chutney

Peel and finely chop the garlic and onions, and put both into a bowl. Peel, then grate the fresh ginger and add to the first two ingredients.

Using a mortar and pestle, a coffee and spice grinder or a heavy-duty plastic bag and a hammer, crush the next five ingredients together. Heat them in a large, heavy-based pot until fragrant, then add the cinnamon and turmeric, and heat through. Add 2 tablespoons of the oil, then the onion mixture, and cook for about 5 minutes.

Measure and add the remaining ingredients, including the rest of the oil. Bring to the boil and simmer for about 1 hour, stirring frequently.

Pour hot chutney into clean, heated jars and top immediately with boiled screw-top metal lids.

Spiced Apricot Sauce

This sauce has a fresh flavour because it doesn't need hours of cooking. To get the texture I like best, I chop the fruit in the food processor before I cook it rather than food processing or sieving the sauce after it is cooked.

3 cloves garlic
1 kg fresh apricots
2 teaspoons cumin seed
1 teaspoon coriander seed
2 cups sugar
2 teaspoons salt
1 teaspoon mustard powder
1 teaspoon ground cloves
1/8 teaspoon cayenne pepper
2 cups vinegar

Chop garlic and apricots roughly then, using a food processor, chop until fine (process in 2 batches for best results).

Lightly roast cumin and coriander seeds in a dry frypan. Grind with a mortar and pestle or in a coffee grinder.

Put all ingredients into a large saucepan and boil for 30 minutes, stirring frequently to make sure the sauce on the bottom of the pan does not 'catch' and spoil the flavour of the sauce. Ladle into hot bottles which have been boiled for 5 minutes with their metal screw tops. Makes 1 litre.

Note: Especially good with plainly barbecued chicken and lamb.

Maharajah's Chutney

This is delicious, unusual and very popular. You can add the sultanas whole, chopped finely, or chopped coarsely. I like it best when I use sultanas which have been coarsely chopped in the food processor. The coarsely chopped sultanas thicken the mixture slightly, so it spreads well on crackers and sandwiches, but they still are in big enough pieces to give the chutney an interesting texture.

10 plump garlic cloves, chopped
500 g onions, chopped
walnut-sized piece fresh root ginger
1 tablespoon black mustard seed
5 small dried chillies
2 teaspoons fenugreek seed
3 tablespoons coriander seed
2 tablespoons cumin seed
1 tablespoon cinnamon
2 teaspoons turmeric
1/2 cup oil
2 tablespoons salt
2 cups malt vinegar
2 cups sugar
500 g sultanas
2 lemons, grated rind and juice

Weights and Measurements

All recipes in this book have been test-cooked. The conversions given here are proportionate measures to enable you to convert a recipe from metric to imperial and are approximate. Standard level metric cups and spoon measurements have been used throughout this book.

The oven temperature chart below is a guide only. To be absolutely sure of good results, always refer to your own cooker instruction book.

Ounces to Grams

Imperial	Metric
½ oz	15 g
1 oz	30 g
2 oz	60 g
3 oz	90 g
4 oz (¼ lb)	125 g
8 oz (½ lb)	250 g
12 oz (¾ lb)	375 g
16 oz (1 lb)	500 g (0.5 kg)
24 oz (1½ lb)	750 g (0.75 kg)
32 oz (2 lb)	1000 g (1 kg)
3 lb	1500 g (1.5 kg)
4 lb	2000 g (2 kg)

Liquid measures

¼ cup	62.5 ml
⅓ cup	83 ml
½ cup	125 ml
1 cup	250 ml
4 cups	1 litre
¼ teaspoon	1.25 ml
½ teaspoon	2.5 ml
1 teaspoon	5 ml
*1 tablespoon	20 ml

*in NZ, USA and UK 1 tablespoon = 15 ml
in Australia 1 tablespoon = 20 ml

Imperial equivalents

600 ml	1 pint (2⅓ cups)
1 litre	1 pint 12 fl oz (4 cups)

Thermostat Setting

	F°	C°
very slow	250	120
slow	300	150
moderately slow	350	180
moderate	400	200
moderately hot	425	220
hot	450	230
very hot	475	250

Measures of Length

in	mm	cm
¼	5	.5
½	10	1.0
¾	20	2.0
1	25	2.5
2		5.0
3		8.0
4		10.0
6		15.0
8		20.0
10		25.0
12		30.0

Cake dish sizes

6 in = 15 cm
7 in = 18 cm
8 in = 20 cm
9 in = 23 cm

Loaf dish sizes

9 x 5 in = 23 x 12 cm
10 x 3 in = 25 x 8 cm
11 x 7 in = 28 x 18 cm

Recipe Index

Page numbers in bold denote photographs